Routledge Revivals

Victorian Comics

The Victorians are usually painted as prim, proper and repressed. Yet it was in Victoria's Britain that the comic paper was born and her subjects eagerly devoured their 'Penny Dreadfuls' and 'Comic Cuts'. Originally published in 1976, this first ever compilation of Victorian comics is culled from England's largest collection by its curator Denis Gifford. In these pages many forgotten figures of fun (such as Ally Sloper, Chokee Bill, Airy Alf and Bouncing Billy) live again, not to mention such notorious episodes as the assault on the Albert Memorial by the Ball's Pond Banditti and the capture of Pretoria by Weary Willie and Tired Tim.

This book is a re-issue originally published in 1976 and contains comics from the Victorian era. The language used is therefore a reflection of its time and no offence is meant by the Publishers to any reader by this re-publication.

Victorian Comics

Denis Gifford

First published in 1976
by George Allen & Unwin Ltd

This edition first published in 2023 by Routledge
4 Park Square, Milton Park, Abingdon, Oxon, OX14 4RN

and by Routledge
605 Third Avenue, New York, NY 10017

Routledge is an imprint of the Taylor & Francis Group, an informa business

© 1976 George Allen & Unwin Ltd

All rights reserved. No part of this book may be reprinted or reproduced or utilised in any form or by any electronic, mechanical, or other means, now known or hereafter invented, including photocopying and recording, or in any information storage or retrieval system, without permission in writing from the publishers.

Publisher's Note
The publisher has gone to great lengths to ensure the quality of this reprint but points out that some imperfections in the original copies may be apparent.

Disclaimer
The publisher has made every effort to trace copyright holders and welcomes correspondence from those they have been unable to contact.

A Library of Congress record exists under ISBN: 0047410027

ISBN: 978-1-032-31276-7 (hbk)
ISBN: 978-1-003-30970-3 (ebk)
ISBN: 978-1-032-31429-7 (pbk)

Book DOI 10.4324/9781003309703

Ally Sloper's Half-Holiday 164; 18 June 1887 (W. F. Thomas)

LOPER'S HALF-HOLIDAY.

JUNE 18, 1887.

BY HER MAJESTY, JUBILEE DAY, JUNE 21ST, 1887.

rthur Sullivan, His Grace the Dook Snook, Mrs. Langtry, W. J. Penley, George Grosmith, Henry Irving, Lord Charles Beres-
ren, Tootsie Sloper, Tottie Goodenough, Phyllis Broughton, Mrs. Sloper, W. Terriss, Alexandry Sloper, Jubilee Sloper, Charles
ke of Cambridge, H.R.H. the Prince of Wales, the Right Hon. W. E. Gladstone, the Elder McNab, Snatcher, and Toddles.

Victorian Comics

The Funny Wonder 191; 26 September 1896 (Tom Browne)

Ally Sloper's Half-Holiday 130; 23 October 1886 (W. G. Baxter)

Victorian Comics

Denis Gifford

FAMOUS COMIC POSTERS.—No. 6.

WHAT would the nation do without its Queen? Worse: What would the Queen do without her COMIC CUTS?

London GEORGE ALLEN & UNWIN LTD
RUSKIN HOUSE · MUSEUM STREET

Big Budget 154; 26 May 1900 (Ralph Hodgson)

ACKNOWLEDGEMENTS

All the illustrations in this book, save for a few photocopies, come from the collection of the author. Acknowledgement is made to the I.P.C. Publications (Juveniles Division) who hold the copyright in many of the Alfred Harmsworth comics.

For the sake of authenticity throughout this book the comics have been reproduced without any touching up or other doctoring. The reader will find that in some instances the captions are faded, since the comics are between seventy-five and a hundred years old.

For Pandy

(No connection with the Pandora Publishing Co.)

First Published 1976

This book is copyright under the Berne Convention. All rights are reserved. Apart from any fair dealing for the purpose of private study, research, criticism or review, as permitted under the Copyright Act, 1956, no part of this publication may be reproduced, stored in a retrieval system, or transmitted, in any form or by any means, electronic, electrical, chemical, mechanical, optical, photocopying, recording or otherwise, without the prior permission of the copyright owner. Enquiries should be addressed to the publishers.

© George Allen & Unwin Ltd 1976

ISBN 0 04 741002 7

Filmset and printed Offset Litho in Great Britain by Cox & Wyman Ltd, London, Fakenham and Reading

CONTENTS

The Comic Paper	page 6
The Comic Hero	27
The Comic Kid	55
The Comic Animal	66
The Comic Age	78
The Comic World	106
The Comic War	120
The Comic Artist: *index*	141

Ally Sloper's Half-Holiday 317; 24 May 1890 (Archibald Chasemore)

The Comic Paper

MR COMIC CUTS AT COURT

The Uncrowned King of Comic Journalism presenting a copy of his Saturday Edition to the Queen of Great Britain and Empress of India—God bless her! (Ratts! This is orl tommy rott, gentile reeder. The old 'un's only bin at Court wunce, and then he cum home forty shillins short.—B. Winkle, Orfis-boy to the *Funny Wonder*!)

The original caption to the cartoon on the front of *The Funny Wonder* No. 191 dated 26 September 1896—the cartoon which appears on page 1 of this collection —sums up the story of the Victorian comic paper. British enterprise, British business, British patriotism, British humour. It also celebrates British style, for it was drawn by Tom Browne, the cartoonist who created British comic technique. Originally invented to bring low-cost laughter to the less than literate, plus profits to their publishers, comic papers continue in like vein to this very day: one of the more enduring institutions of the Victorian Age. The rough and the tumble, the bash and the splash, the black-eye and the bandage, are as basic to today's *Beano* as to yesterday's *Chips*. The cop and the robber, the kid and the teacher, and tucked away in corners, the dog and the mog, still fight the good and funny fight eighty years on and bid fair to make their century. Comics are a continuing saga, and there lies the rub: there is no point in their history where we can pick up a particular paper and proclaim it Comic Number One. This makes comics intriguing to the historian, infuriating to the collector. But begin they did, and their roots are squarely within that era of yesterday labelled Victorian.

Queen Victoria succeeded William IV on 20 June 1837; four years later *Punch* was born (17 July 1841). It was the latest and, as it turns out, the longest lived, in a long line of comic magazines inspired by the French *Figaro*. These weeklies were of a higher class than the illustrated broadsheets of the streets: more middle than working. The humour was satirical, the tone political, and there was none of the 'squinting eyes, wooden legs, and pimpled noses' which, according to William Makepeace Thackeray, 'form the chief points of fun' in the 'outrageous caricatures' of C. J. Grant, mainstay of such broadside series as *Every Body's Album* (1834). A marriage of the two classes came with the publication of an obvious *Punch* pinch, *Judy* (1 May 1867). The format followed the tradition for weekly magazines, a handy $8\frac{3}{4} \times 11\frac{1}{4}$ in., with one page given over to the topical

Ally Sloper's Half-Holiday

BEING A SELECTION, SIDE-SPLITTING, SENTIMENTAL, AND SERIOUS, FOR THE BENEFIT OF OLD BOYS, YOUNG BOYS, ODD BOYS GENERALLY, AND EVEN GIRLS.

No. 1.]   SATURDAY, MAY 3, 1884.   [ONE PENNY.

cartoon, as such caricatured comment had been called since *Punch* published John Leech's 'Substance and Shadow' on 15 July 1843. It was not until *Judy* was three months old that something remarkable occurred within her pages.

It was called 'Some of the Mysteries of Loan and Discount' and it was a full page story told in pictures (p. 26). It was contributed by a prolific parodist and penny dreadful purveyor whose rough sketches were finished in ink for him by his seventeen-year-old French wife. Within two years Charles Henry Ross was the Editor of *Judy*, Mrs Ross ('Marie Duval', née Isabelle Émilie de Tessier) his leading cartoonist, and their character Ally Sloper a national institution. Ally, with his weekly adventures in pictures, qualifies as the first true British comic strip hero. He was the first to appear in comicbook format (*Ally Sloper: A Moral Lesson*, a paperback reprint collection of 216 pages and 750 pictures was published in November 1873, price one shilling), the first to have his own comic paper (*Ally Sloper's Half-Holiday* published weekly from 3 May 1884), and the longest lived in comic history (the last regular *Half-Holiday* was on 29 September 1923, the very last published in Scotland in 1949).

The magazine format was not to prove the ideal one for the comic paper. It was James Henderson who unfolded the average sixteen pages into an eight-page tabloid, $11 \times 16\frac{1}{2}$ in., and called his fifty-fifty combination of text and cartoons *Funny Folks*, 'A Weekly Budget of Funny Pictures, Funny Notes, Funny Jokes, Funny Stories'. One penny every Monday, No. 1 was published on 12 December 1874, and carried an editorial introduction in verse.

> Funny Folks! 'Tis just a budget,
> Full of pictures, jokes and fun,
> Pleasantly and not unkindly
> Showing what is said and done.
> Funny Folks, it seems to tickle,
> Funny Folks presents to view
> As a camera that all things
> To its Funny focus drew.

On the front was a large topical cartoon by John Proctor, and inside a 'Comic Fancy Page' by Montbard, together with three strip cartoons, two of them foreign. The text pages included a detective story parody, 'The Horrible Disclosures of S. Probe', and a humorous column by 'Mrs Grundy'. Thus in shape, size, and style, *Funny Folks* founded the form that the British comic would cling to for three-quarters of a century. The basic difference was, of course, that like all its immediate ilk, *Funny Folks* was a picture paper for the adult, not the child.

No. 1.—GRATIS COPY.   No. 2 will be published, THURSDAY, MARCH 12th, 1885, at 2 o'clock. No more Free Copies.
OFFICES: 153 FLEET STREET, LONDON, E.C.

JACK and JILL

An Illustrated Weekly Journal for Boys and Girls.

No. 1.]　　　　　SATURDAY, March 7, 1885.　　　　　[One Penny.

James Henderson was the first of the new breed of working man's publisher. He specialised in providing low-priced fun, fact and fiction, with no aspirations towards the rarer air of the monthly magazines, yet a cut above the broadsides of Seven Dials and the penny dreadfuls of Edward Lloyd. Henderson had entered publishing in Manchester with *The Weekly Budget* (1861), and then set up in London at Red Lion House, Red Lion Court, as a specialist in juvenile literature: *Our Young Folks' Weekly Budget* ran, with several variations in title, from 2 January 1871 to 31 October 1896. Henderson's biggest rival in popular publishing was George Newnes, who pioneered scrap-book journalism with his phenomenally successful *Tit-Bits* (22 October 1881). Immediately imitators abounded (*Rare Bits, Funny Bits, Pick'd Bits*), Henderson included. But where Newnes pasted up paragraphs of text, Henderson clipped pictures: *Scraps*, subtitled 'Literary and Pictorial, Curious and Amusing' (29 August 1883), was a collage of cartoons and comic strips cut from *Harper's Weekly* and *The Judge* (New York), *Fliegende Blätter* (Munich) and *La Caricature* (Paris). Henderson also avoided the *Tit-Bits* image by making *Scraps* match *Funny Folks* in size and shape. The popularity of these Henderson twins inspired the Brothers Dalziel to produce their 'Selection, Side-splitting, Sentimental, and Serious, for the Benefit of Old Boys, Young Boys, Odd Boys generally, and even Girls'. They called it *Ally Sloper's Half-Holiday*.

Gilbert Dalziel had taken over *Judy* in 1872. The great engraver had promptly raised the old girl's sights, aiming at the *Punch* market, but was careful not to interfere with the career of her star performer. The paperback reprints had become annual best-sellers with *Ally Sloper's Comic Kalendar* (1876-84), supplemented by *Ally Sloper's Summer Number* (1880-4) and such special editions as *Ally Sloper's Guide to the Paris Exhibition* (1878) and *Ally Sloper's Book of Beauty* (1880). Ally's own paper was the logical consequence. It is said that from it Dalziel made £30,000; what Ross made, if anything, is unrecorded. The first issue had two small Ross-Duval cartoons; both of them were reprints. In fact, all the Sloper strips in the *Half-Holiday* were reprints, many going back twenty years. It was the Sloper cartoons that made the *Half-Holiday*, huge panels that filled most of the front page and exploded across the entire centre spread every Christmas (back end-paper). Cartoons that set Sloper in the thick of any and every event of the day, from christening his latest offspring in honour of the Queen's Jubilee (p. 78) to being dubbed Baron Sloper of Mildew Court (front end-paper). This 'new look' Sloper was created by W. G. Baxter, a brilliant cartoonist born in America, raised in Buxton, and trained on the Manchester weekly *Momus*. His caricatures of local notables and occasions raised his status to Joint Editor, but

JACK'S JOURNAL

An Illustrated Weekly Miscellany for Everybody.

In continuation of "**JACK and JILL.**"

| ol. IV.—No. 115.] | SATURDAY, May 14, 1887. | [One Penny. |

he still found time to freelance for Dalziel's *Judy*. When *Momus* closed in 1883, Dalziel brought Baxter to London, and his first front page cartoon graced the tenth number of *Ally Sloper's Half-Holiday*. Ally himself did not appear until three weeks later, when Baxter drew him in full grog-blossom bloom holding a 'Hyde Park Demonstration' beneath a banner which proclaimed for the first time his famous slogan, 'Ally Sloper, the Friend of Man'. This was quickly condensed to 'F.O.M.', and soon a whole string of impressive but suspicious initials followed (p. 2). A much envied set was 'F.O.S.', the Friend of Sloper award, which was pictorially presented on the back page every week from 19 November 1887. The first went to G. H. Chirgwin, the White-Eyed Kaffir; the 963rd to Charles Ross, Junior, who wrote a weekly piece under the pseudonym of 'Tootsie Sloper'. Dalziel's other contribution to the comic was order. Instead of the jumble that was *Scraps*, Sloper readers could be sure of finding their favourite features in fixed spots in the paper. Text, spotted by small cartoons, was relegated to the alternate spreads of pages 2-3 and 6-7, making a refreshing break from the massed cartoons that filled the front, back, and middle. James Brown's slapstick Scots saga of 'The McNab', another hold-over from *Judy*, ran as a strip across the bottom of page 4; above these caber capers was 'Distinguished People Interviewed by A. Sloper' (anyone from J. L. Toole to Swinburne to the Prince of Wales was fair game for fun); opposite was the topical comment cartoon, 'Our Weekly Whirligig'. Dalziel's well-laid centre spread would become a characteristic feature of the British comic.

'The Largest Penny Illustrated Paper in the World' was the claim Davis and Marshall made for their *Illustrated Tid-Bits*, a sixteen paged penn'orth which began on 4 October 1884, and began again on 17 January 1885 as *Illustrated Bits* after George Newnes brought a law suit. There were other dramas during this comic's career, including changes of Publisher, Editor, policy, and size; but it also introduced the first deliberate attempt to discover strip cartoonists. Editor 'Bimbo' ran a Grand Prize Comic Tableaux Competition offering one pound for 'six small comic tableaux illustrating a story'. And so, besides creating a new field for artists, Bimbo coined the earliest known term for the comic strip—and acquired a supply of them at less than going rates!

The first comic specifically designed for children was *Jack and Jill*, published by W. Long on 7 March 1885. A charming scrapbook of sketches and verse, it had Edward Lear on the back page and was a total failure. With the eighth issue the subtitle was changed from 'An Illustrated Weekly Journal for Boys and Girls' to 'An Illustrated Journal for Everybody', and from 14 May 1887, the title itself was changed to *Jack's Journal*. It was now clear to publishers and purchasers that there existed two distinct classes of humorous journalism, the *Punch* school—both

SNACKS

A JOURNAL OF HUMOUR, ROMANCE, COMIC CUTS, AND ANSWERS ON EVERYTHING.

Vol. I. No. 3. SATURDAY, JULY 20, 1889. [ONE PENN

Pick-Me-Up (1888) and *The Jester* (1889) were in this magazine tradition, although their aim was comedy not comment—and the *Funny Folks* format—*Snacks* (15 June 1889) was clearly a comic. The most significant thing about this mainly reprint paper was its sub-head: 'A Journal of Humour, Romance, Comic Cuts, and Answers on Everything.' But before explaining this significance, to keep in strict chronology mention must be made of *Laughter*, 'A Weekly Budget of Mirth, Wit and Humour', published as a short-lived, sixteen-paged, half-size comic from 15 February 1890.

James Henderson employed a great many freelance contributors to help fill the columns of tiny type between the line-blocks. One of these hacks was a fifteen-year-old Irish lad called Alfred Charles William Harmsworth. This son of a barrister had so rapid and adept a turn of the pen that within two years he was made Assistant Editor of a boy's paper called *Youth* (1882). In 1885 Harmsworth went to Coventry to work on papers published by Iliffe & Sons, returning later to London to serve in the office of George Newnes. The continuing success of *Tit-Bits* and the comparative ease of its weekly compilation was inspiration to his ambition, and one month before his twenty-third birthday, Harmsworth, helped by his brothers, issued his own magazine from a small room on the first floor of 26 Paternoster Row. He called it *Answers to Correspondents*, and the print run for his No. 1, dated 12 June 1888, was 13,000. Within a year the circulation had almost quadrupled. Eager to enlarge, Harmsworth cast around for another success to simulate. He found it in *Funny Folks* and *Scraps*, published by his first employer, James Henderson. And so on 17 May 1890, from a slightly more salubrious address in Fleet Street (No. 145), Harmsworth issued the first edition of his second venture.

Comic Cuts was clearly not the first British comic, as its publishers would constantly claim throughout the fifty-three years of its life. Indeed, it looked like any of the many comics then on the market, and not only in size and format: it reprinted cartoons and strips that Henderson himself had reprinted five or more years before! Even its title was unoriginal: *Comic Cuts* had appeared in the sub-heading of *Snacks* the previous year, and anyway was standard trade jargon for a humorous engraving on a printing block: a 'cut' that was comic! But the new paper had the Harmsworth touch, the same touch that had made *Answers* a real rival to *Tit-Bits*: he sold it at half the regular price: 'One Hundred Laughs for One Halfpenny!' Wrote Harmsworth in his first editorial:

Remember the following facts about *Comic Cuts*. It is as large as any penny paper of the kind published; this you can prove by measurement. It employs the best artists, is printed on good paper, is published every Thursday, will give

10

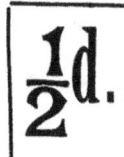

big prizes, is the first halfpenny illustrated ever issued, and has plenty of money behind it. How is it possible for anyone to provide an illustrated paper, containing nearly fifty pictures, over eighteen thousand words, and many valuable prizes, for a halfpenny? Well, it is possible to do it, but that is all.

Cheap reprints helped, of course; even the text was lifted from back numbers of *Answers*! But a small notice in No. 3 promised some hope for the future.

WANTED!

ORIGINAL SKETCHES

FOR

"COMIC CUTS."

HANDSOME PAY OFFERED.

PROFESSIONAL ARTISTS ONLY NEED APPLY.

The first Professional Artist was Roland Hill, and his first strip made the front page of No. 4. *Those Cheap Excursions* (p. 18) is typical of Hill's strips depicting the suburban scene. Next came Oliver Veal, who worked in the then-fashionable silhouette style (p. 19). Solids soon proved unsuitable for the cheaply printed comics, and Veal evolved a freer form that found him a full-time career as a strip cartoonist.

If Harmsworth's ha'porth had not actually started the comic in Britain, it had certainly started the comic boom. Number 1 sold out; wrote Harmsworth, 'I was at Nottingham the first day *Comic Cuts* appeared, and on asking for the paper was unable to get one in the whole town'. Number 2 sold out, too, and by the time Harmsworth sat down to compose his 'What the Editor Says' for No. 3, other publishers were busily preparing cut-price comics. 'Well, gentlemen,' wrote Harmsworth, 'I have got a good start, and you will have to put in several thousands of pounds, much hard work, and a few other attributes of success before you get ahead of the first halfpenny illustrated.' Secretly Harmsworth got busy on another comic of his own.

Funny Cuts hit the newsagents' shops on 2 July 1890, published by Trapps, Holmes & Co, neighbours and rivals of James Henderson in Red Lion Court. This eight page ha'penny was edited by Gordon Phillip Hood, whom Trapps and

ILLUSTRATED ½d CHIPS ½d

No. 1.—Vol. I. [Entered at Stationers' Hall] PRICE ONE HALFPENNY. [Transmission Abroad at Book Rates] JULY 26, 189

Holmes introduced thus: 'We promise our readers that our Editor is the funniest man on earth. He is a very Samson or Sandow of humour. He is irresistible'. He was also pretty smart with the scissors, pasting up his pages with cartoons clipped from those American magazines which Harmsworth and Henderson had unaccountably missed. But by No. 16 (25 October) finances had improved sufficiently for Hood to give over his entire front page to Alfred Gray, an old hand from *Judy* and *Sloper* (pp. 42–3). *Funny Cuts* was a great success and ran for thirty years, clocking up 1,566 issues. Harmsworth's answer, his companion to *Cuts*, was a horrible failure and folded after six weeks. Or, rather, unfolded. . . .

Here you are, then! Here is the Editor with his bottle of hair-restorer by his side (N.B. He is a strict teetotaler so you needn't make any nasty insinuations), and his false teeth hung carefully on the gas bracket. Observe the kind and amiable expression on his face; look at the bags of gold in the corner.

Hardly Harmsworth, except perhaps for the bags of gold! He had called his new paper *Illustrated Chips*, taking the title from *Choice Chips*, a cheap imitator of *Tit-Bits*, vintage 1884. For once the famous Harmsworth touch failed him. He had halved his tabloid *Comic Cuts* to produce a smaller paper of more pages, sixteen for a halfpenny. It seemed a good idea, but the format of *Punch*-style weeklies was not popular with the working-class readers of comics. *Chips*, as it was colloquially called, was born on 26 July 1890, and quickly born again on 6 September. This No. 1 'New Series' was back in the tried and true format of *Comic Cuts*, an eight-page tabloid. On 6 June 1891, the paper turned pink, and stayed pink for fifty years. It was pink again when it died, hand in hand with its white paper partner, on 12 September 1953.

The Victorian comic age arrived with a rush. Henderson produced *Snap-Shots* on 9 August 1890, one month before *Chips* unfolded into tabloid. Henderson, unable to halve his price, doubled his page-count: *Snap-Shots* boasted sixteen picture-packed pages for one penny. It was a scrapbook, but an honest one. The sub-head read, 'Humorous Pictures and Amusing Reading chiefly from Advance Proofs of Current American Papers by Exclusive Arrangement'. By 1900 *Snap-Shots* reversed the *Chips* evolution by halving its page size, upping the count to twenty-four, and printing a Club Edition on art paper for twopence: it had become a magazine. Another reprint comic, this time back at a halfpenny, was *Skits*. Number one came from the British Publishing Company, yet another denizen of Red Lion Court, on 27 June 1891. *Skits* closed after twenty-three issues. Murray Ford did much better with *The Joker*, notching up a six-year run from 18 July 1891. The front page featured a single cartoon signed 'Frank C'.

starring spotty, spectacled 'Tony Green' and his embarrassing escapades with his comely cousins, Lottie, Tottie and Dottie. *The Joker* was even racier than *Sloper*, and ran pin-up sketches of such stage sweeties as Miss Harriet Vernon in the series 'The Joker's Lady Friends'. Henderson tried a flier in the old broadside style: *The Comic Pictorial Sheet* was no more than an unwieldy one-page reprint, published twice weekly from 29 September 1891, in several different sizes. At the other end of the paper scale came his *Comic Pictorial Nuggets* (7 May 1892), a sixteen-page halfpenny half-tabloid that soon became *Nuggets* (26 November). This one was a reprint of reprints, proclaiming its source as 'From *Scraps, Snap-Shots, Young Folks,* and the publications of Red Lion House for Over Thirty Years'. Trapps, Holmes & Co. brought out their second title on 6 July 1892. *The World's Comic* (p. 107) was reputedly edited by Grandad Twiggle, but clearly the Samson or Sandow of Humour was at work again, and from No. 29 they admitted the Editor to be Gordon Phillip Hood. The comic ran for sixteen years before combining with its companion, *Funny Cuts*.

All this comical activity by no means daunted Harmsworth, and on 30 July 1892, appeared Alfred's first editorial for number one of *The Wonder*.

> Well, it is out at last. The new halfpenny paper you have heard so much about is in your hands. Don't you think it is a wonder? Did you ever see a paper like it before, one as big, with so many pictures, or with pictures so good, and all for a halfpenny? Why, it is positively giving you a twopenny paper for a quarter of its value!

Unfortunately Harmsworth's editorial effusions failed to wash with the reader: *The Wonder* was neither a novelty nor a bargain. It was large, matching the once-folded broadsheet of the daily newspaper, but at four pages it contained only marginally more than its twice-folded companion comics. Harmsworth's continual effort to produce something different was certainly creditable, but he was wasting his time. Just as his half-size *Chips* had failed to catch on, so did his double-size *Wonder*, and after a run of twenty-seven weeks he was forced to revert to his winning format of *Comic Cuts*. With a slight retitling to emphasise the comical content, *The Funny Wonder* began again on 4 February 1893. It was an immediate success and ran, with slight changes of title and format, to that familiar, final date of 12 September 1953.

George Emmett, a boys' paper publisher, entered the field on 8 August 1892, but left again after a mere six weeks: *Jolly Bits* ('from Jolly Books') lacked the comic touch. Much more fun was *Larks!* (1 May 1893), 'founded and conducted' by Gilbert Dalziel (p. 57). He issued it from 'The Sloperies' (99 Shoe Lane, E.C.)

with the advice that 'a penn'orth of Sloper and a ha'porth of *Larks* every week ought to make the British Nation happy!' It did, for nine years. The power of the comic was felt in the land: Charles P. Sisley's 'Artistic Weekly' *Up-To-Date* suddenly switched to the new funny format on 12 August 1893, after a near-fatal flirtation with illustrated news. *The Champion Comic* appeared on 9 January 1894, as a companion to *The Joker*, but had to be incorporated with its more successful partner exactly two years later, in spite of the offer of '10s a week paid to you if laid up by an accident'. Henderson brought out *Varieties* as a follow-up to *Nuggets* on 12 May 1894. At thirty-two pages for one penny it was a bargain bundle, but of reprints. Its magazine size was matched by Trapps, Holmes, who published *Side-Splitters* on 6 August 1894: sixteen pages for a halfpenny. Alfred Gray, their staff cartoonist, was made Editor, but the venture failed, and nine weeks later it was incorporated into *The World's Comic*.

Alfred Harmsworth had his failures, too. He tried out a story paper in the comic format, calling it *The Boy's Home Journal*. After five disastrous issues he switched text for sketches and began it again as *The Comic Home Journal* (11 May 1895). He played doubly safe by linking the 'new' paper with *Chips*, featuring portraits of the Editor, Cornelius Chips, and the office boy, Philpot Bottles, in the heading, and pretending that the renovated comic was really 'the Friday Edition of *Chips*'. The stunt worked, and the comic ran for nine years. Gimmicks were the order of the day, and when C. Arthur Pearson entered the comic market on 19 June 1897, his *Big Budget* (p. 82) went one better than Henderson's *Nuggets* and *Varieties*, which each contained a sixteen-page supplement of fiction. *Big Budget*'s catchline was 'Three Papers for a Penny!' First came an eight-page comic, then the eight-page *Comrades' Budget*, and lastly the eight-page *Story Budget*: twenty-four tabloid-size pages for one penny! It could not last, they said, and it did not: but only four pages and the sectionalisation had been lost by the end of the year. Under the excellent editorship of Arthur Brooke, *Big Budget* settled down to a twelve-year stretch.

The Joker lost his sauce and his 'r', becoming *Jokes* with effect from 20 January 1898 (p. 74); the change extended his life by but twenty-two weeks. Now George Newnes, Harmsworth's old rival, entered comics and produced *The Halfpenny Comic* on 22 January 1898 (p. 48). His experienced touch ensured success, and the paper ran for nine years. *Comic Bits*, from the Unity Publishing Co., did less well. The first issue came out on 19 February 1898; the last ten weeks later. Pearson's companion to his *Big Budget* met with little more success, despite the apparent advantage of being hooked to the top comedy personality of the period: *Dan Leno's Comic Journal* (26 February 1898) lasted ninety-three weeks (p. 87). *The Monster*

Comic (15 March 1898), a ha'penny pink'un put out by the Sketchy Bits Company, reached No. 14 before it closed. It fell victim to the new nomenclature: comic it was, 'a comic' it was not. It was a magazine.

In America the comic was a late but fast developer. Like the British originals, it evolved out of the weekly humour magazines, *Puck*, *Life* and *Judge*. Unlike the British originals, it was not sold. Joseph Pulitzer and James Gordon Bennett gave their comics away with their rival Sunday papers, the New York *World* and *Herald*, from 1894. Strips appeared among the jokes almost immediately, but regular characters did not develop until 1896, and did not 'take over' the comics until 1900. Where the American comics beat the British was in the use of colour. They were in full colour from the start, while colour did not come to the British comic until 12 September 1896. It was, as might be expected, an Alfred Harmsworth enterprise. The Special Autumn Edition of *Comic Cuts* was a history-making mess. 'Printing in colours in this country has hitherto been a failure', editorialised Harmsworth, and this twelve-paged, four-coloured, twice-the-price edition proved that the tradition of the British printer was holding true. However, Harmsworth had faith and persisted in his experiments. Coloured Christmas numbers followed, with occasional specials for the companion papers, *Chips* and *Wonder*, but it was left to his rivals, Trapps and Holmes, to publish the first regular comic in colour. They called it, of course, *The Coloured Comic* (p. 36). It first appeared on 21 May 1898, and 'Mr C. C.' wrote from 'The Editor's Colour Box': '*The Coloured Comic* has been a long thought-out project. It has necessitated the outlay of huge capital, so large indeed that I wonder where it all comes from. Sometimes I think it can be that the proprietors have been to the Klondyke and struck oil!' Only the front page was printed in full colour, and only for seventy-two weeks, although the comic itself ran to 1906. It managed to justify the continued use of its title by printing in blue instead of the standard black.

James Henderson produced his first proper comic on 2 July 1898, and it was another 'first': instead of four pages of pictures and four of stories, he put pictures on every page. *Pictorial Comic Life*, 'The Amusing Picture Paper for the People', became the last new title of the Victorian era. The Queen died on 22 January 1901; *Pictorial Comic Life* on 21 January 1928. Clearly, comics had come to stay.

Pictorial Comic-Life

EVERY MONDAY. No. 1. For Week Ending July 2, 1898.

½D

8 Pages of Pictures. ½d.

The Amusing Picture-Paper for The People.

Printed and Published by James Henderson, at Red Lion House, Red Lion-court, Fleet-street, London.

IN CANNIBAL-LAND.—AN EXPLORER'S CLEVER DOG.

"My master has a biscuit in his pocket. Wish I had it," thought the dog.

"Oh, lor'! no more biscuits! Here's an end of me!"

"Might as well die game."

"Never seen a dog stand on his tail, evidently."

"How does a somersault strike you, old boy?"

"Dear me! I never thought I'd live to see that biscuit."

[This Series will be continued next week.]

THE ANNUAL BEANO.

Come what may, 'Arry must take his annual "beano." (Note—'Arriet strictly prohibited, this journey.)

Pictorial Comic-Life 1; 1 July 1898

Illustrated Chips 396; 2 April 1898 (Tom Browne)

½d. Comic Cuts. ½d.
ONE HUNDRED LAUGHS FOR ONE HALFPENNY.

No. 4. Vol. I.] Registered.   ONE HALFPENNY WEEKLY.   [June 7, 1890.

THOSE CHEAP EXCURSIONS!

Jones and Brown resolve to take a holiday. "There's an excursion, and I'm going down to Margate to get a good blow," said Jones to Brown, as they left the office. "Take my advice—don't!" said Brown.

Jones starts—5 a.m.—without breakfast.

Going down—five hours of this for Jones, who doesn't smoke.

He just has time for "a good blow."

And then the return journey—all night on a "siding."

Brown sleeps till noon—

Dines early and well—

Takes a walk over Hampstead Heath in the afternoon—

His girl to the play in the evening.

(*Tuesday morning.*) Brown fresh and smiling! Jones limp and lank!

Comic Cuts 4; 7 June 1890 (Roland Hill)

The characteristics of the comic are so universal that it seems pointless to detail them. Yet they took longer to evolve than did the comic paper itself. *Funny Folks*, the first, never got around to establishing a regular character, despite the obvious appeal of Ally Sloper in his *Half-Holiday*. Baxter and Thomas never drew Sloper as a strip, despite Ally's seventeen-year career in picture story form in *Judy*. Tom Browne drew several strips a week for six years before he tried repeating characters: then Weary Willie and Tired Tim became part of British history.

PICTURES! JOKES! STORIES!

No. 1 (New Series). [Entered at Stationers' Hall.] PRICE ONE HALFPENNY. [Transmission Abroad at Book Rates.] Sept. 6, 1890.

"IN THE SPRING (ALSO IN THE SUMMER) A YOUNG MAN'S FANCY LIGHTLY TURNS TO THOUGHTS OF LOVE."

"We must fly to-morrow! My father's consent can never be obtained," she said. | "Farewell, dearest! To-morrow, at eight o'clock, in Gipsy Lane!" said Adolphus. | But the irate parent overhears the conversation, and determines to thwart the wicked design. | Having made every preparation for a hasty flight, Adolphus is there at the appointed time.

"Ha! she comes! I know her footsteps so well. My happiness is now complete!" | "My dearest!" he cried in the blindness of his joy. | But he quickly discovers he has made a mistake— | And returns a crestfallen man, and evidently the worse for his adventure.

Illustrated Chips 1; 6 September 1890 (Oliver Veal)

A BIG CRICKET MATCH as reported by the Sporting Correspondents.

Comic Cuts 10; 19 July 1890 (Roland Hill)

½d. Comic Cuts. ½d.
ONE HUNDRED LAUGHS FOR ONE HALFPENNY.

No. 51. Vol. II.] Registered.   ONE HALFPENNY WEEKLY.   [May 2, 1891.

 CLEVER ARTISTS SHOULD SUBMIT WORK TO THE EDITOR OF "COMIC CUTS,"
Enclosing large stamped envelope for return, in case of rejection. (IMMEDIATE PAYMENT.)

THE EDITOR AND THE WOULD-BE COMIC FIEND.

(1) The Editor was sitting in his sanctum knocking off a few hundred jokes for COMIC CUTS, when a head was thrust round the door, exclaiming: "Sir, I have here a comic drawing suitable for—" "Begone!" replied the Editor impatiently.   (2) Scarcely had the Editor resumed his pen when the head appeared through the window, saying: "Sir, I have here a comic drawing suitable for—" "Vanish!" replied the Editor sternly.   (3) The Editor once more turned to his work, muttering angrily, when he was again assailed by the head, which this time appeared down the chimney crying: "Sir, I have here a comic drawing suitable for—" "Wretch, leave me!" answered the Editor savagely.

(4) Sure of having effectually rid himself of his unwelcome visitor, the Editor dashed off a score of jokes, when he was maddened to desperation at beholding the head through the skylight, saying "Sir, I have here a comic drawing suitable for—"   (5) It was more than the Editor could bear. Dragging the man down, he stabbed him to the heart with his paper-knife. But even while his life's blood ebbed away, he muttered: "Sir, I have here a comic drawing suitable for—"   (6) And every night as the clock strikes twelve a shrouded skeleton appears to the Editor, saying in sepulchral tones: "Sir, I have here a comic drawing suitable for—"

Comic Cuts 51; 2 May 1891 ('F.L.')

MR. COMIC CUTS AND THE WOULD-BE COMIC FIEND.

1. The Editor was sitting in his sanctum, knocking off a few hundred jokes for COMIC CUTS, when a head was thrust round the door, exclaiming: "Sir, I have here a comic drawing, suitable for—"
"Begone!" cried Mr. C. C. impatiently.

2. Scarcely had the Editor resumed his pen, when a head appeared through the window, saying: "Sir, I have here a comic drawing, suitable for—"
"Vanish!" replied the Editor sternly.

3. Mr. C. C. once more turned to his work muttering angrily, when he was again assailed by the head, which this time appeared down the chimney, crying: "Sir, I have here a comic drawing, suitable for—"
"Wretch, leave me!" answered the Editor savagely.

4. Sure of having effectually rid himself of his unwelcome visitor, Mr. C. C. dashed off a score of jokes, when suddenly he was maddened to desperation at beholding a head through the skylight, saying: "Sir, I have here a comic drawing, suitable for—"

5. It was more than Mr. C. C. could bear. Dragging the fiend down, he stabbed him to the heart with his paper-knife. But even while his life's blood ebbed away, he muttered: "Sir, I have here a comic drawing, suitable for—"

6. And every night as the clock strikes twelve, a shrouded skeleton appears to Mr. C. C., saying in sepulchral tones: "Sir, I have here a comic drawing, suitable for—"

Comic Cuts 441; 22 October 1898 (Roland Hill)

WARNING!
If the editors of other papers continue to copy COMIC CUTS jokes, cases like the following will be numerous.

He saw it in COMIC CUTS first, and he nearly laughed the top of his head off.

Then he found it in *Prig'd Bits*. It was so good that he laughed again, though not so violently.

He was thunderstruck when he found that the editor of *The Joke Stealer* had cribbed it. "It's a little too much," he muttered; "I'm tired of that infernal joke."

A week later he was fairly staggered, for he found that *Snips* had slightly altered it, and labelled it original.

Finally, he took up a local paper, and that joke; but before he could read it reason gave way, and they led him off to the lunatic asylum, and chained him down in the padded room.

Comic Cuts 10; 19 July 1890

Big Budget 150; 28 April 1900 (Ralph Hodgson)

Pictures might be of any size or shape, or be arranged in 'artistic' designs (p. 22); neatly ruled frames did not become common until 1898, and then were generally confined to front pages. Stories were narrated in 'librettos', squibs of text that ran underneath each panel. When a rare attempt was made to tell a story in pictures alone (p. 23), it was supplemented by explanatory paragraphs on an inside page.

The Joker 277; 22 October 1896

The Halfpenny Comic 74; 17 June 1899 (Ernest Wilkinson)

The balloon was a device as yet unborn. Ernest Wilkinson created a brief vogue for explanatory placards (p. 24), while 'Yorick' (Ralph Hodgson) was the first to flirt with actual speech within the frame (p. 25). Yorick, forced to follow Tom Browne's line when that artist abandoned comics, helped to consolidate the style that by 1900 was becoming the standard: clean, neat, open linework spotted with well-balanced blacks, plus plenty of action. Action, simple slapstick in pictures: this was the completely new thing comics had to offer, the thing which the humorous magazines lacked. To understand a *Punch* cartoon you had to read a caption as long as a short story. Although it helped to read the captions in a comic, you could pick up the gist of the joke with no more effort than the flick of an eyeball. No wonder children liked comics, and no wonder, once that section of the reading public became financially viable, the children took them over.

HAPPY IKE HAS SOME AWFUL SHOCKS TO THE SYSTEM.

1. FIRST WE HAD SOME GRAND TURTLE SOUP

1. You see Ike was just thinking how bootiful a sausage and mashed would go down.

2. THEN SOME LOVELY FRIED SOLES

2. When that feller in the funny hat started talking about a big dinner

3. AFTER THAT A DELICIOUS FOWL AND CHIPS

3. He and a pal of his had had the day before.

4. THEN SOME BEAUTIFUL SADDLE OF MUTTON, BAKED POTATOES AND SPROUTS

4. And Ike stood it as long as he could, but at last

5. AND FINISHED UP WITH BOB CIGARS AND COFFEE!

5. He collapsed all of a heap. "Take me away," he gasped. "I do feel so bad."

6. "I wouldn't go froo dat again for a million quids," he moaned.

Big Budget 160; 7 July 1900 (Ralph Hodgson)

1. "Hech! but the MacHaggis has found a bonnie lot of fowls," murmured the MacWeedrap, as he espied his old enemy strolling home through the night. "I suspect the laird will find his fowl-hoose empty in the morning."

2. But he changed his tone next morning when he found that, with the exception of the old rooster, all his own birds were missing. "Eh, mon, this is MacHaggis's work!" he groaned. "I might have known it."

3. "But nae doubt he'll coom back for this birdie, an' he can hae it, and welcome." "Oh, canny, mannie," smiled the other Mac, who saw the plot. "It occurs to me that it's not me that'll be blown up."

4. Then did the wicked MacHaggis get a worm, and tie it to a long, slow match. "Puir, sweet wee birdie!" he chuckled, "jeest get a wriggler into your gizzard, and dinna heed the string." "Ay," replied the cock-a-doodle; "I wilt."

5. Now MacWeedrap was on the watch, and directly he saw the rooster running round in a circle with a long line attached, he thought it'd get choked. "Come back, ye pesteeferous crow!" he yelled. "I mean to catch ye!"

6. Well, MacWeedrap caught more than he bargained for. At the precise moment that bird went BANG, and away went both. "Farewell, ma bonnie braw laddie!" yelled MacHaggis; "gi' my respects to the mon in the moon."

Illustrated Chips 509; 2 June 1900

1. As Iky Mo and ALLY SLOPER could raise no more money on their own account, what was more natural than that they should start a Loan Office, and lend money to others.

2. Iky began with a splendid notion: "Let's advertise Loans without the least inquiry or the slightest security."

3. And didn't the public respond?

4. Only ALLY's great idea of "Twopence for a form of application" didn't seem to answer.

5. "Capital, one million." View of the interior of the iron safe.

6. This is a "Meeting of the Board."

7. And this is a faithful likeness of a pair of boots with which Mr. SLOPER became personally acquainted. N.B.—*They had a would-be borrower's feet in them too at the time.*

Judy; 14 August 1867 (Marie Duval)

The Comic Hero

Alexander Sloper, F.O.M. (Friend of Man), was known as Ally for short and for good reason: fond of that quarter-day caper called the Moonlight Flit, he was forever sloping up an alley. Born on 14 August 1867, of mixed parentage (writer C. H. Ross, artist Marie Duval, Mrs Ross), he spent seventeen years in *Judy* strips before W. G. Baxter remodelled him for thirty-two more years as a cartoon in *Ally Sloper's Half-Holiday*. Here his hobnobbing with royalty reformed the 'Old Rumfoozler' as little as did his regular arrests by the peelers. If not the first ever comic strip hero, certainly the first ever anti-hero, Ally established the outlaw as everybody's favourite funmaker. More, he operated in tandem with Isaac (Iky) Moses (Mo), thus establishing the double act, too.

ARREST OF SLOPER.

"A raid has been made on 'The Sloperies,' and Poor Papa has been arrested by the Police. Personally, I know very little of the matter; but, from what the Dook tells me, it appears that, for some time past, Mr. Moses has been conducting a Betting Club in one of the upstairs rooms at '99.' The Police are in no way to blame; the affair was forced upon them by the Home Secretary. There wasn't a dry eye amongst the Constables engaged, and the whole thing has caused a deep gloom throughout the Force. It is hoped, however, that 'ALLY SLOPER'S CHRISTMAS HOLIDAYS' will appear on the 8th, as already announced."—TOOTSIE.

Ally Sloper's Half-Holiday 344; 29 November 1890 (W. F. Thomas)

Illustrated Chips 298; 16 May 1896 (Tom Browne)

'He Knew How To Do It' was the title of Tom Browne's first published work, printed in James Henderson's comic *Scraps* on 27 April 1889. A significant title to a significant cartoon: an eight-panelled strip of slapstick paperhanging. Tom, born 1870, was a poor Nottingham apprentice, and the thirty shillings Henderson sent him was equal to three months' salary in the print shop. Tom answered Harmsworth's ad for artists and soon chucked up the litho trade for *Comic Cuts*. His 'Innocents on the River', just another set for *Chips*, caught the public's fancy, and 'Weary Waddles and Tired Timmy' soon took over the entire front page, slightly rechristened 'Weary Willy and Tired Tim' (p. 29). Tom modelled them on his own heroes, Don Quixote and Sancho Panza, and later turned them into a strip, too (p. 30). Disreputable double acts caught on. Tom's 'Airy Alf and Bouncing Billy' (p. 82), bicyclists (Tom's favourite pastime), soon turned tramp and even met their mirror-image rivals (p. 31). Footpads hit the front page highway in comic after comic.

No. 471. Vol. XVIII. (New Series.) [Entered at Stationers' Hall.] PRICE ONE HALFPENNY. [Transmission Abroad at Book Rates.] SEPTEMBER 9, 1899.

A WILD NIGHT'S ADVENTURE WITH SPRING-HEELED JACK.

1. "Willy, dear boy, how do I strike you?" warbled Tim. "Strike me—throw me—pinch me—bust me! but you're just too wonderful for words!" smiled Willy. "Are you Spring-heeled Jack, or a winged microbe? Oh, I know now! You're the Human Bat what we read about in the 'Wonder.'"

2. And sure enough that vampire had a giddy time of it that evening on the common. "Wough! I am the ghost of your fat uncle!" roared the monster. "Don't run, children; let's stop and play together." "No you don't," roared the crowd, "we never had a uncle—at least, not with a dial like that! Ta-ta!"

3. So the Bat popped in to see how Sophie and Jack were getting on with their spooning. "Coughdrops and liver pills!" yelled the chap; "may I be stewed in hair-oil if it isn't the old 'un!" "Yow! Ho-oh! Hellup! Take it away!" twittered the maiden. "I'll never marry with anything like that in the family."

4. Once more across the common the Bat spotted a few of his old enemies. "Oh, you beauties!" he whistled. "I've got you now, and if I don't knock spots out of your earholes may I be sugared!" "Don't touch us, Mister Bat," yelled the cops; "we're too young to die."

5. But if the cops were nervous the night-birds weren't, and they flocked up to see what the row meant. "'Ere, what do you call yourself?" piped the old crow. "Let's have a taste! Peck, peck!" "Willy," shrieked Tim, "'ere are some nasty dicky-birds hurting your little pal."

6. Poor Willy was in too much of a tangle to go to the rescue, and presently a crowd of yokels came along with a gun and other hurtful instruments. "Come, birdie, come, and fly with me," snorted Tim, as they pitched him into the pond. "I am coming, gentle Timmy," whined Willy. Then the cold waters closed over them! But they'll appear, as per, in CHIPS next Thursday.

Illustrated Chips 471; 9 September 1899 (Tom Browne)

The Unrecorded Adventures of Don Quixote de Tintogs and Sancho Panza, His Faithful Servant.

INTRODUCTION.

NOW it is well known that Don Quixote was an old-fashioned gentleman who gave himself up so wholly to the reading of romances that a-nights he would pore on until day, and a-days he would read on until it was night; and thus, by sleeping little and reading much, the moisture of his brain was exhausted to that degree that at last he lost the use of his reason.

A world of disorderly notions, picked out of books, crowded into his imagination; and now his head was full of nothing but enchantments, quarrels, battles, challenges, wounds, complaints, amours, and abundance of stuff and impossibilities, insomuch that all the fables and fantastical tales which he read seemed to him now as true as the most authentic histories.

Having thus lost his understanding, he unluckily stumbled upon the oddest fancy that ever entered a madman's brain, even in a comic paper; for now he thought it necessary, as well for his own honour as the service of the public, to turn knight-errant, and roam through the whole world, armed cap-à-pié, and mounted on his steed, Rozinante, in quest of adventures.

The adventures of this remarkable person and his simple, faithful servant, Sancho Panza, have been related in a famous work, but it has been reserved for us to convey to the world the true narration of the exploits of these worthies as they *really* occurred, together with some spicy tales concerning Rozinante, the horse, the ass, and the entirely-forgotten dog, Trust, who will now appear for the first time. These adventures will appear (ONE EACH WEEK). We shall proceed to correct some existing delusions upon the best-known adventures of Don Quixote, and tell first—

THE TRUE STORY OF THE TOSSING IN THE BLANKET.

1. One day as the weary knight approached an inn he saw, to his astonishment, his servant, Sancho Panza, being tossed in a blanket. Filled with wrath, he bade them stop.

2. But as they took no notice, he hastily mounted his trusty steed (Rozinante, the catsmeat vendor's hope), but with the wrong leg up first.

3. Consequently, setting spurs to his trusty steed, he entered the yard in a not too dignified manner. "Put old Tintogs in as well," they cried.

4. And in he went into the blanket. Just then Sancho's ass strolled in. "In with the ass," they cried.

5. No sooner was the ass in the blanket when some-one cried, "In with the boneshaker."

6. So in went pussie's hope, followed by the dog, Trust, just for luck—tossing "heads and tails," as it were.

Comic Cuts 440; 15 October 1898 (Tom Browne)

Newsagents will find it pays them to display The Big Budget. 1d

GRAND FOOTBALL SERIAL STORY JUST STARTED.

Vol. V. No. 122.   WEEK ENDING SATURDAY, OCTOBER 14, 1899.   Price 1d.

AIRY ALF AND BOUNCING BILLY MEET THEIR GREAT RIVALS.

1. Airy Alf and Bouncing Billy had blued all their coin, and were padding the hoof to the B.B. office, to knock a few bobs out of the Editor. "Billy," chirped Alf, "ole B.B.'s knocking 'em all with that noo football serial, ain't he?" And Billy was jist about to open his little potato-trap to reply when—

2. The rivals came face to face. "G-r-r!" gasped Weary Tim and Tired Willy. Is it them or their ghosts?" And the Budget boys gurgled: "Is it troo, or is it onli a nightmare?"

3. Then the first act of the tr-r-agedy commenced. "A-h-a!" hissed Tired Willy, as he biffed Billy neatly. "I've been wanting to talk to you for a long time." And Weary Tim sweetly purred: "Take that, you slab-sided son of a bottle-nosed slop."

4. You will observe, dear readers, that the argument is still proceeding. "Billy," gasped Alf, "how's our side?" And Billy's voice arose from the scrimmage, and warbled: "Arf a mo, cocky. I'm just tryin to git a bit of 'is ear orf."

5. At length youth began to tell. "Oh-er," gasped Weary Tim, who had got the ogles of the knock-out. "I feel sorter run down." And Tired Willy chipped in: "I fink I've had enuff, cockies. Let's play at somfing else, shall we?"

6. The great battle was over, and the Budget boys were on top. "Alf, my noble warrior," said Billy, "it was a good scrap, wasn't it?" "Get out," chortled the long 'un, "Why arsk 'em wot they fink about it." And two mournful moans arose on the air, as the victims groaned: "Let's 'ave one more gargle afore we die."

Big Budget 123; 14 October 1899 (Ralph Hodgson)

THE ADVENTURES OF CHOKEE BILL AND AREA SNEAKER. } SERIAL STORY, BEGINNING BELOW.

OUR COLOURED NUMBER LAST WEEK BROKE ALL RECORDS. — ANOTHER COMING SOON.

Comic Cuts. ½d

ONE HUNDRED LAUGHS FOR A HALFPENNY.

No. 355. Vol. XIV.]   Registered.   ONE HALFPENNY WEEKLY.   [February 27, 1897.

CHOKEE BILL AND HIS NOOMATIC INJYRUBBER BOOTY-BAG (continued next week).

1. "Did I never tell yer nuffink abart me noomatic booty-bag, Mr. Edditter? No? Well, 'ere goes, then. Yer see, the cops had got voosed ter me cawpit-bag, an' so me and Snaggums (the Skinny Kid) invented a noomatic injyrubber booty-bag, wot 'ud go in yer pocket, an' would stretch ter ercommodate any quantity of booty yer could collar.

2. "Yer'll 'awdly berlieve me, Mr. Edditter, but the werry fust bit o' swag I collared in that there booty-bag wos a private gemman, a watch-dorg, an' a perliceman. 'Ow did I do it? Well, like this 'ere. I'd just farstened me booty-bag onter a winder-ledge, so's I could drop me swag in froo the winder—

3. "When a dorg as I'd never noticed made a sudden honslaught onter me. In I bolts froo the winder.

4. "Fortchernetly, the dorg dropped a bit short, and fell whack inter me noomatic bag.

5. "But not before he'd wakened the party in the 'ouse wiv his barkin' an' 'owlin'. The consequence wos, I had ter bolt for that winder again in a jiff, wiv the 'ouseholder an' a cop at me 'eels.

6. "In course I made a jump ter clear me noomatic booty-bag; but the 'ouseholder pawty, knowing nuffink abart it—

7. "Went a swatter into it, onter the poodle, wot wos a-whiskin' raand inside.

8. "Well, that wos a bit o' luck orlright; but when the cop comes an' stawts gittin' out backards way fer safety, an' drops smack in onter the poodle an' the 'ouseholder pawty, I see'd me charnce; an' just as he dropped—

9. "I tied up the marth o' me injyrubber booty-bag and cavorted safe as 'ouses! Worn't it a corker?"

Comic Cuts 355; 27 February 1897 (Frank Holland)

AUBREY 'AWKINS AND GINGER JONES TRY TO NICK THE CROWN JEWELS.

1. Aubrey and Ginger were clean pebbly-stoney, as per, and being badly in want of a hundred thousand quid to buy toffee with, they thought they'd go to the Tower of London and sneak the crown jewels. "Ha! ha!" murmured Aubrey, as they got to the entrance; "but we must be wary!" "Wot ho!" said Ginger.

2. They managed to find their way up to the bedroom of the chap who had the keys, and Aubrey sprang at him like a cannon-ball with the jumps. "So ho, villin!" he yelled, "you are in our power, and must lead us to the room where the joos be!" "Yus; and look slippy," chipped in Ginger.

3. That yeoman of the guard, being an obliging chap, said he would. "'Tis well, caitiff. We will follow thee," said Aubrey. "Lead hon, Macduff!" grinned Ginger. "And look 'ere—no hurts!"

4. When they got to the Tower, Ginger thought he'd like to make the acquaintance of the cove in the meat-tin on horseback. But the chap didn't like being interfered with, and he nearly squashed the dinner out of the Auburn One. "Yeow! chuck it!" yelped Ginger. "You've tore my evenin' dress!"

5. At last they got to the Jewels Room, and Aubrey ordered the yeoman to do up as many of the valuables as they could carry in a brown-paper parcel. "Aub," cried Ginger, "wot price me? S'lute yer k'ng, carn't yer!" "Rats!" said Aubrey.

6. But they got stucked in after all; for that yeoman chap managed to give 'em the wrong parcel. "Don't think much of your jooler's shop," grinned Ginger, when they undid the parcel. "Which shall we sell first—the Royal Diamond Cat or the Himperial Golden Dog?" (They don't seem to have much luck, do they?—ED.)

The Funny Wonder 268; 19 March 1898

The World's Comic 295; 23 February 1898

Funny Cuts 404; 2 April 1898

HENRY T. JOHNSON'S GREAT STORY, "DANDY JIM." (SEE PAGE 2.)

THE ½d Coloured Comic ½d

No. 1. Vol. I.] ONE HALFPENNY. [MAY 21, 1898.

OF THE SAME OPINION.

HOW FROG-FACED FERDINAND AND WATTY WOOL WHISKERS GOT A MONKEY.

(1) It was this way. The sailor left his box outside the pub and Frog-faced Ferdinand and Watty Wool Whiskers couldn't resist it, they really couldn't, you know. So they pinched it.

(2) And took it home and opened it, when "Jumping Johnson!" out sprang a monkey, and after tickling Watty in the tater trap, it tried to pull his whiskers.

(3) Then it went for Ferdinand, and tried to pick his pocket in quite a professional style, which fairly won Watty's heart.

(4) "Good old Monkey Brand," shrieked Watty, "yer one o' the boys. Come ter me arms me long lost brother."

(5) Then they thought they'd take a stroll and faked the monkey up in the landlady's togs. "Looks spiffing," says Froggy. "Only wants a veil," says Whiskers.

(6) In the park they met a masher. "Strike me spicey," says Wool Whiskers, "if he ain't mashed on the monkey. We oughter make fools out o' this."

(7) And that merry monkey kept it up, and managed to pinch the masher's watch, while Froggy pinched his wipe.

(8) Then the masher stole a kiss, "whiskers," he yelled, in dismay, that settled him, and didn't—

This is a Pippin, and no error. We all like it—so will you.

The Coloured Comic 1; 21 May 1898

BERTIE BOUNDER AND ALGY ARDUP STRIKE SOME COLD HARD TROUBLE AGAIN.

1. That gentleman guffing away there is Signor Alberto Bounderi, with his celebrated phonograph. Hist! dear readers, you recognise him? Well, don't blow the gaff then. "Walk up, ladies and gents," he shouts, "yer just about to 'ave the greatest treat of the season. Me famous funnygraph is now a-going to yap out a few select hairs, the same which it 'as performed before the German Hemperor and all the corned feet of Europe. No coppers taken, and silver sniffed at. Walk up."

2. "'Ere you have the 'Soldiers of the Queen,' as sung by the Hero of Mafeking himself. 'Ark to the lovely notes of that magnificent barrowtone voice." "It's a fair coughdrop," shouted the crowd, and the pieces began to dribble in. "Well, this looks like a bit of sugar for the bird," chortled Bertie Bounder, "wot price kippers for breakfast termorrow?"

3. When the phonograph started reciting the Charge of the Light Brigade, the enthusiasm was immense, and the spondulicks simply poured in. "My eye," crooned Bertie to himself, as he bowed before the delighted crowd, "this beats a whelk stall all hollow." But, unfortunately, he did not notice that nasty inquisitive sailor man at the back. "I wonder 'ow them funnygraphs work. I've a great mind to just lift this one up and ——"

4. And just as Bertie was wallowing in the little quidlets, with his back towards the phonograph, the sailor lifted the top off the machine, and—gave the whole show away; for 'twas Algy a-working that funnygraph all on his own. "You now get the chance of a lifetime, people," cooed Bertie, as he stuffed the oof into his pockets, "to 'ear the lovely voice of the most beyootiful singer of the present day——" "You bloomin' frauds," howled the crowd, "we'll goffer yer."

5. And then the crowd took them to the end of the pier, and gave them a nasty, rude, rough push into the cold, kerewel sea. "Oh, save me," screamed Algy, "save yer boyhood's pal. I'm so delicate, I shall be sure to die if I get drownded. Oh, why don't somebody throw me a lifeboat." "'Elp," shrieked Bertie, "man overboard. Take yer dirty boots out o' me weskit."

6. Fortunately, the mud wasn't very deep just there, and so they managed to get ashore, and made tracks for the station, with the crowd full pelt after them. "Bertie," puffed Algy, "they're catching us up. Why didn't yer listen ter me when I told yer ter keep honest?" "Rats!" panted Bertie. "It's you wot's the cause of orl my troubles."

Big Budget 161; 14 July 1900 (Charles Genge)

THE ASTONISHING STORIES OF JIMMER SQUIRM AND SPOOKY THE SPRAT.

1. DEER MISTER EDDITTER.—We wos burglin'. I know it wos norty, but we wos doin' it. Jimmer 'ad worn his trotter-boxes darn till there wos 'ardly enaythink left of 'em but the lace-'oles, an' there wos nuthink for it—'e 'ad ter 'ave a noo pare of 'oof-cases some'ow. So we busts inter a boot-shop. Well, we'd 'ardly got nicely in when a cop spots us an' meks for the winder ter koller us.

2. "Spooky," ses Jimmer, "we're lorst!" "Lorst be 'anged," I ses. "You go lose yer face! I've got a little wheeze wot'll worry that cop a bit. Wot we wornt is cover, a'n't it?" "Yus," ses Jimmer. "Well," I ses, "wot price this 'ere boot?" "Spooky," ses Jimmer, "geenius ain't the word fer you. You're a korf-drop." "Never mind wot I am or wot I ain't," I ses, "you foller me."

3. "Right o!" ses Jimmer: an' in 'arf a tick we wos tucked inside that boot as nice an' comfy as if we wos in a third class kerridge on a Bank 'ollerdy excurshun. "Sh-sh-sh-sh! 'ere's the cop; don't bayave," ses Jimmer. "I can't," I ses, "yer squeedgin' too mutch." Then the cop garsps "lost, gorn? !Gorn? Well, this is the narstiest knock I've ever 'ad !" "I'd giv yer a narstier if I 'ad a brick," I wispers.

4. Then 'e blinks up an' darn, an' every time he looks up we ducks darn inter the boot. At larst 'e guv it up an' scooted orf. "I thort 'e wos goin' ter 'ave a fit," ses Jimmer, larfin'. "So 'e is," I ses. "An' a regler parerlettic one too. Darn yer, git art of 'ere, Jimmer! Look slick! Now un'ook that boot! That's it!" An' in a cupple o' ticks, Mister Edditter, we 'ad that boot orf its 'inges, an' wos reddy for bizness.

5. "Wot's the game now, Spooky?" ses Jimmer, fairly flabbergarsted. "That's the game," I ses, pointin' to the copper darn below. "An' mind yer sees as yer pots him properly." Just then we 'ears the peeler marmurin' "Well, I dunno wot's a-comin' over me." "No," I ses, "but I know wot's a-comin' over yer—this," an' we drops the boot.

6. "Well, yer sed as yer'd give 'im a fit, Spooky," ses Jimmer, "an' I reckon you've guv 'im a booty." "Yus," I ses, "'e might ha' bin measured fer that boot, mightn't 'e?" An' after that we does our little bit o' bizness an' clears art. But yer shu'd ha' heer'd the langwidge wot was a-buzzin' inside that boot, Mister Edditter, it wos orful. Well, as I sed ter Jimmer, "Jimmer," I ses, "I can't stay 'ere an' listen to it. We must go." So we went.—Yoorstrooly, SPOOKY THE SPRAT.

Big Budget 176; 27 October 1900 (Frank Holland)

THE STARTLING STORIES OF JIMMER SQUIRM AND SPOOKY THE SPRAT.

1. DEAR MISTER EDDITTER,—We've 'ad a werry near go this lawst week! We wos in the country for 'ealth an' rekerryation (an' ennyfink else we cud lay our 'ands on), an' wos just trottin' orf wiv a foo turmuts when the farmer an' a cop cums bunkin' arfter us.

2. There's no dowt we'd ha' bin kollered too, if we 'ad'nt suddingly cum to a wire fence, when I struck the idea o' yoosin' it as a kattypult, wiv the turmuts for hammynition (as per picter).

3. "Gimme me my turmuts!" yells the farmer, as 'e cums bouncin' up. "Right o! There yer are!" I ses, an' I biffs 'im wiv a big 'un right on the boco.

4. Over 'e goes, an' up cums the cop. "And over them turmuts," 'e 'owls.

5. "Suttingly, yer lawdship," I ses, an' I 'ands 'im one on 'is chivvy, an' 'e flops over wivout so much as sayin', "Thenk yer."

6. O' coarse arfter that evveryfink wos orlright, and orf we toddled
Yourz truly, SPOOKY THE SPRAT.

Big Budget 179; 17 November 1900 (Frank Holland)

1. "See here," said Hiram B. Boss to the City man, "there's buried treasure in your back garden at home—£10,000 of it. Gimme a cheque for £500, and I'll give you the plan. I've got ter catch a train."
"Ha-ha! not me," laughed the City man.

2. Hiram saw he was not to be had. "I rather calculate I'll have to make it a bit easier for him," he murmured. So he bought about five bobs' worth of brass counters, and buried them in that chap's back garden.
But he was observed.

3. And presently, two imps of boys came and dug up the box with those counters, and took it away, and in its place put a box they had borrowed from their little brother, who was away from home.

4. The next time Hiram turned up in that City man's office, he said: "See, I'm back again! I missed that train; but if you'll promise me the £500 the minute I shows you the gold, I'll take yer to yer condemned garden and hold the lantern while yer digs it."
"That's better," said the City man. "Have a cigar."

5. "Ho, ho!" said the City man, "the gold, the gold, the red, red gold!" when he dug up the box.
"Got that £500 in notes?" said Hiram.
"I've only got to undo the catch," went on the City man, "and wealth is mine, beyond the dream of a policeman!"

6. But it wasn't wealth he got. No; it was a nasty, ugly, little Jack jumper which the imps had borrowed from their little brother.
My! didn't Hiram have a happy, happy time!

The Funny Wonder 259; 15 January 1898 (Jack B. Yeats)

EPHRIAM BROADBEAMER, SMUGGLER, PIRATE AND OTHER THINGS

1. A terrible storm was raging at Ephriam's birthplace, and the townspeople were alarmed for the safety of the boats. "Only one thing for it!" yelled Ephriam to the Mayor. "Pour oil on the troubled water."

2. The Mayor happened to be an oil-merchant, and so he took Ephriam's tip, and altogether they spilt about a thousand gallons on the waves. It had the desired effect, though.

3. And that was where Ephriam came in. As soon as the oilers had cleared off, he scooted down to the beach, got his boat, and scooped in gallon after gallon of the oil, for, as you know, oil always floats at the top of water.

4. He made a good bit out of it; but, of course, he must needs go and spoil himself by being greedy. He hadn't got enough to satisfy himself, so he went up to the Mayor again. "There's another storm a-comin', and we wants more oil," he said. He didn't get it—the Mayor had been watching him.

The Funny Wonder 284; 7 July 1898 (Jack B. Yeats)

Jack B. Yeats' style was as different from Tom Browne and his school as his crooks were from Tom's tramps. Perhaps this might be expected of the son of a poet (William Butler Yeats). Like Browne, Yeats later turned away from the black linework of comics to the coloured brushwork of paintings; unlike Browne, Yeats was never imitated. His artistry stands alone in British comics. 'Hiram B. Boss' and 'Ephraim Broadbeamer' are clearly unique crooks, just as his 'Chubb-Lock Homes' (p. 45) is out of the ruck of comic coppers—traditional game in the Victorian comic, traditional game today. Comic editors often appeared as comic heroes (p. 46) or guest stars (pp. 47–8); proprietors, too (p. 17).

THE SWADDY, THE SLAVEY, AND THE SLOP.

I.—Cooky and the Parrot were At Home to their pet P'liceman, but just when the cold mutton was about to tighten his belt—

II.—Horror of horrors! a Guardsman's shadow darkened the windy blind. "Oh, lor, Robert, if 'taint my cousin Dick," shrieked the fair but frail Cook. "Inter the pantry, quick."

III.—It was all very well; but, Jerusalem, worn't it a squeeze; they just managed it in time, though, and that's all.

IV.—All went well till that wretched Parrot up and opened his mouth with one fatal speech!!!

V.—The son of Mars went for that cupboard straight; and a good deal of fur and feather started flying around.

VI.—They went at it like catamounts till they collected the bits which belonged to 'em, and got them gone. They haven't called on that fickle hearted Cooky since; not much!!!

Funny Cuts 34; 28 February 1891 (Alfred Gray)

Funny Cuts 41; 18 April 1891 (Alfred Gray)

THE KOPS CARN'T COP THE B. B. KID.

Big Budget 96; 15 April 1899 (Frank Wilkinson)

The Funny Wonder 1½d

THE SATURDAY EDITION OF "COMIC CUTS."

No. 219. Vol. IX. [New Series.] ONE HALFPENNY WEEKLY. APRIL 10, 1897.

ADVENTURES OF CHUBBLOCK HOMES AND SHIRK, THE DOG DETECTIVE.

1. Chubblock Homes, the great detective, had hunted everything, from gamps to lost hearts, but he never hunted little pet pigs before. "Find him!—our Adolph—our little curly-tailed cherub—and great rewards are yours! That's his paster; let Shirk sniff it!" So said the guardian of Adolph, the Baby Pig.

2. The chase began. What is yonder sign? Ham is cheap. Alas; poor Adolph. "On, on! let us hear the wust!" gurgled the guardian down in his slippers.

3. "No, no!" said the ham-and-beef man, "I have not cooked your little Adolph; but I saw a man go by with him towards the dog show." That was enough. On went Chubblock Homes and Shirk. The owner of Adolph was tired; so he rode.

4. At the dog show. The robbers had escaped with Adolph; but an artist for a daily paper had made a sketch of the little pet. The judges had thought he was a foreign pug dog, and given him first prize. Shirk, upsetting the owner of the pig, took a good sniff at the drawing. Then the chase was resumed—

5. Hullo! a lot of ladies fighting. "Say," cried Chubblock Homes, "tell me, young man in the button, what is the cause of yonder battle?" "Oh, it's only the mothers fighting over the way the first prize went in the baby show." Oho! the baby show. A suspicion flashes through Chubblock's mind.

6. The way the first prize went—it went to little Adolph. They thought the petsie, ducksie, ickle sing was a baby. But the thief escaped, taking those prizes with him.

The Funny Wonder 219; 10 April 1897 (Jack B. Yeats)

The Funny Wonder 246; 16 October 1897 (A. H. Clarke)

Big Budget 100; 13 May 1899 (Ralph Hodgson)

The Halfpenny Comic 1; 22 January 1898 (Tom Browne)

THE SPUDKINS-BALMPOT FEUD; or, THE CHRONICLES OF MUDBOROUGH-ON-THE-MIRE (continued).

1. "Deer Sir,—I'm that mad I could eat Hezekiah Spudkins raw. Arter all 'e did ter me larst week me heart wos softened terwards 'im cos the parson come an' torked that evenin' abart brotherly love an' sich. Arter a tremenjous struggle wi' meeself (which I'm 'avin in this picter), I ses 'I'll forgive him.'

2. "An' I goes right out, an', puttin' me dooks out, 'Hezekiah,' I ses, 'gimme yer 'and, an' from now let us be brothers!' Well, at that he was quite took back. 'Balmpot, old boy,' 'e ses, arter 'e'd done bein' took back, 'I will.'

3. "An' as 'e gripped my dook we both turned away an' swollered summat in our throats—lumps they wos. 'An' now,' I ses, as me voice shook, 'let all be forgotten. Wotever blaggardly treatment I've received from you, Hezekiah, I forgives.'

4. "'Blaggardly treatment?' 'e ses, sudden. 'I ain't aware, Augustus, as I was ever gilty of any sich!' Worn't that paltry, Mr. Edditer, after my 'andsome treatment of 'im?

5. "'Then I'm a liar, am I?' I ses, my dander risin'. 'You insultin' scoundrel, I'll gouge yer eye out!' 'You'll wot?' he says. 'Dare to, an' I'll——'

6. "'You dare me, do you, you villainous brute!' I'll grind you to pulp!' I ses.

7. "An' wiv me British blood fairly up, sir, I flew at 'im, an' scratched an' bit 'im like a wild cat.

8. "An' if the perlice 'adn't interfered, sir, I'd 'ave shown 'im the stuff I wos made of, if I'd 'ad to chaw 'im up to do it.—Yoors trooly, AUGUSTUS BALMPOT."

The Funny Wonder 259; 15 January 1898 (Frank Holland)

MR. BODGER PUTS IN A PANE OF GLASS.

1. "We'll soon have this new pane of glass in, my dear," said Mr. Bodger. "No need to have a glazier blundering about the house over a little job like that. You see, we just chop out the old glass and putty—

2. "Then we take the new pane of glass—so, and put it in!"

3. But instead of fitting it in, Mr. Bodger pushed it right through, and it fell out into the street.

4. And, as luck would have it, it dropped on the head of Beery Benjamin.

5. Beery Benjamin couldn't miss a chance like that. In about two-fifths of a second he was inside Bodger's house demanding compensation.

6. And Mr. Bodger had to pay. And, what's more, he gave that window-mending to a glazier after all!

The Funny Wonder 255; 18 December 1897 (S. W. Cavenagh)

THE HANDY MAN'S TELESCOPIC EYE.

1. "Make me a glass optic," said the one-eyed party; and the Handy Man said "Right!"

2. "Well," says the Handy Man, "first I tried a red-blue-and-green glass marble; but he said it was too fancy for him. Jist then my eye dropped on my ole telescoop. So I says, 'Whacher think of a telescopic eye?'"

3. "Well, first I redooces the size of my ole telescoop. It took a lot of redoocing with the meat-chopper; but I thought if I got a fiver for the job it 'ud be wuth it."

4. "Then I fixed it in the ole party's empty skylight, and proceeded to paint an eye on the end just like Nater, only more. I had to tie up the ole 'un dooring the continuance of the proceedings."

5. "But at last it was done, and the party, having paid me, clutched hold of my arm and said, 'This is all right! Come and see it work. Observe yonder fishwife,' I observed."

6. "Well, he went up to her, and, 'Is that sole fresh?' says he. 'I have me doubts.' 'By Axelander Pip!' says the fishwife, 'is it fresh? There ain't nothink fresher in the entire ocean!' Then the old party touched the spring, and—"

7. "Let go the telescopic eye, remarking at the same time, 'G-u-r-rh! You wicked story!' Well, it gave the ole fish-party such a turn that, if you ask her if her fish are fresh now, she tells you the exact day last week when they came out of the sea. Fact!"

The Funny Wonder 244; 2 October 1897 (Jack B. Yeats)

Falls and fights are the basis of slapstick, and 'The Spudkins-Balmpot Feud' celebrated nothing but knockabout for weeks on end. Domestic slapstick featuring father was frequent, and first regularised in the weekly adventures of 'Mr Bodger'. Jack Yeats' 'Handy Man' was less helpless, as you might have expected, and A. H. Clarke's 'Wimble' (p. 52) took on a new job every week. Tom Browne widened his horizon with 'Robinson Crusoe Esq' (p. 53); while Charles Genge pinned down a popular type in his 'Bertie Bounder' (p. 54).

"SONS OF THE SEA," Thrilling Complete Naval Stories. See p. 99.

The Halfpenny Comic ½

No. 65. Vol. III.]   Week Ending April 15, 1899.   [One Halfpenny.

WIMBLES'S REMINOOSANCES.

1.—Ho no! It ain't ori sticky toffee bein' a railway hofficial. Frinstance, arter a little amoosement sech as the above, cultivatin' a tenpenny thirst on yer, the party sez "Thanks, o, so much! Take a track! We shall be offly appy to see yer at our little tin chapel on Sundays." And yer can only gurgle: "D'lighted, m'sure," cos yer too dry to say more.

2.—And then there's the old gel wot never couldn't even travel ter the next station without her menagerie, an' sez: "Dear me, Mister Porter, 'ow the little dears do take to yer! Ow remarkable it is that the little creechers can tell people wot is fond of em." Grrrh! A battered brown far this lot, wot yer carn't even impoge on a aumakatic machine.

3.—And then the luggage orfis: people comes in and leaves things while they goes for ter set their watches. One man left a thoughtful-lookin' dorg wot yer wouldn't suspect ennything wuss than chasing cats, an me, innercent like, takes 'im as per usual and leaves 'im with the other bundles.

4.—But, bless yer! When e opens the door agen, except a few odd bits, there weren't nothing but dorg left—not a sign of ennything else. So ter satisfy the people, I tries to work out by jography wot part of the dorg was golfsticks and wot part wos washin' but not bein' a Solomon, I 'ad ter give it up and let 'em settle it peaceably amongst themselves.

5.—Which they wos bizzy doin', when the two thirty hup hexpress comes rattlin' along the metals, and I suddenly spots a hobstacle on the line, which pruved to be a brars button. Heedless of the danger to myself, I jumps down ter remove it——

6.—But alas, too late! an' I got such a uncommon tidy hump on a most wery inconvenient portion, it give me sech a earache I was obliged to resign my position. (NEXT WEDNESDAY, WIMBLES AS A GARDENER.)

The Halfpenny Comic 65; 15 April 1899 (A. H. Clarke)

Comic Cuts 484; 19 August 1899 (Tom Browne)

BERTIE BOUNDER'S LITTLE RIVER PARTY COMES OFF BADLY FOR HIM.

1. BERTIE BOUNDER took Flo and Gertie up the river the other day. Fair dook was Bertie, leaning back in the punt, with his arm round one girl, while the other did the work. The two tired, hot chaps on the bank looked longingly at the punt. "Wot-ho! fatheads!" shouted Bertie quite rudely, "don't yer wish yer was rich and good-looking like me? Don't wear yer boots out too fast walking, cockies."

2. Then when they got out at the Swagger Hotel, the two chaps came up and looked over the fence, and Bertie got ruder still: "Hullo, not dead yet," he chaffed, "wy doutcher come in, have lunch—ain't yer got any ooftish? Ha, ha!"

3. But while Bertie was enjoying himself with the girls, the two chaps thought they'd get their own back, and they moved that notice board and put it just where it would lead Bertie nicely over the weir. "Whoa, there," growled the fat chap, "yer a-shoving me into the river, stoopid!" However, they fixed the board up all right.

4. And when the punt came along, it was Bertie this time who was guiding the noble bark. "Ow," he yapped, as he saw the board, "good job I saw that board, girls, or I should have gone the other way for cert. You trust yerselves to me, dears, and you'll be all——"

5. Wollop! Sp'ash! Whish! *They had reached the weir!* Then the two heroes rushed out and nobly rescued the girls. "Saved, saved, darlings!" they chortled. "Chuck it," and the girls clung. "Oh, why don't somebody save me!" gurgled a voice from the bottom of the river (it was Bertie). "Save yourself," the two chaps called rudely, "you weren't born to be drowned."

6. And when Bertie finally crawled out, the girls were in the punt with those two chaps. "Go 'ome and get yerself wrung out!" the rude fellows sniggered, "we'll look after the girls." And Bertie limped off. (Look out for his last adventure next week. It is a funny one).

Big Budget 114; 19 August 1899 (Charles Genge)

The Comic Kid

Kids and comics were inseparable from the very beginning. Comics, intended for the working-class clerk and artisan, appealed to children because of their visual nature. Now and then editors slipped in 'Something for the Children': Tom Browne's 'Billy Buster the Steam Engine' in *Comic Cuts* for 14 March 1896, was described as 'a tale of a toy engine to be read aloud to the youngsters while they look at the pictures'. When children first appeared in comics, naturally it was as mischief-makers (p. 56). The first child heroes were, of course, as delinquent as their adult equivalents. Gordon Fraser's 'Ball's Pond Banditti' (p. 57) are the great grandfathers of 'Lord Snooty and His Pals', as their names testify: Ticko Scubbins, Gorger Pain, Piggy Waffles, Lurcher Geeson, and Sweppy Titmarsh!

"LARKS!"

"*It appears that the doings of those terrible creatures, 'The Ball's Pond Banditti,' are to be illustrated and described each week on the front page of* Larks! *Poor Pa was naturally curious to make the acquaintance of these gentlemen, so he invited them all to a winkle tea in the back garden at Mildew Court. He has since observed more than once that he always considered Alexandry and Bill Higgins sultry, but they are lamb-like when compared to the 'Banditti.' However, on Monday next, May 1, the First Number of* Larks! *will come out, and as it is only a Halfpenny, there's bound to be a big rush for it.*"—TOOTSIE.

Ally Sloper's Half-Holiday 470; 29 April 1893 (W. F. Thomas)

Funny Cuts 37; 21 March 1891 (Alfred Gray)

Larks! 1; 1 May 1893 (George Gordon Fraser)

JACK SHEPPARD AND LITTLE BOY PINK OFF TO KLONDYKE.

1. Well, Jack Sheppard the Younger and Little Boy Pink didn't do very well at Klondyke last time, so they made another start; but this time they laid in some provisions, same as they'd heard was usual. They took pickles and jam.

2. Well, they went by water, according to the usual style of going to Klondyke, and about dinner-time they got hungry. A little ahead they saw a grizzly bear. "We'll dine on this," says Jack, drawing his catapult.

3. It hit the grizzly fair on the chest, but it didn't stop it; and it wasn't a grizzly at all, but a fat man in a fur coat. On, on he came. "They're desprit when roused," sung out Jack, "Watch me lay him out with pickles."

4. They hit him fair, and stopped his snorting career. "On to Klondyke," says Jack Sheppard. "Onst more we're sailing on the bosom of the misty deep, on to wealth."

5. And they continued to "toot" leaving the grizzly-man-monster dying on his backbone. "Ha, ha," laughed Jack. "Yonder I see it's a lake."

6. Next minute they were there. But it wasn't Klondyke. They'd made a mistake; it was the duck-pond at the back of the "Bald-faced Nag," and their victims were waiting for them.

Big Budget 29; 1 January 1898 (Jack B. Yeats)

Jack Yeats' juvenile delinquents had to be slightly different from the rest, of course. 'Little Boy Pink' sounds innocent enough, but his partner in crime is the junior of no less a highwayman than Jack Sheppard! Their abortive trips to the Klondyke strike a topical touch. Weary Willy and Tired Tim had their juniors, too, and Tom Browne drew them for Cornelius Chips' companion comic, *The Funny Wonder* (p. 59). 'The *Big Budget* Kid' was cast in the mould of an American success, Richard Outcault's 'Yellow Kid', Bowery slang and all. Middle-class delinquents came to comics through Tom Browne, once again riding his favourite hobby (p. 61). Next year he introduced a regular dose of delinquency in the weekly 'Doings at Whackington School' (p. 62). 'Those Terrible Twins' first appeared in the Grand Double Easter Number of *The Halfpenny Comic*. Four weeks later they moved to the front page, ousting the overly adult 'Mr Stanley Deadstone and Co.' (p. 48). Kids may be said to have taken over comics from that fatal date.

No. 284. Vol. XI.   ONE HALFPENNY, EVERY SATURDAY.   JULY 9, 1898.

THE ADVENTURES OF LITTLE WILLY AND TINY TIM.

1. "Willy," murmured Tired Tim, with a smirk, "our sons is 'Chips' of the old block, ain't they?" "Yes, you wicked old jokist, they am," replied Weary Willy; "ain't it Wonder-ful! Well, boys, are you going to join your honourable parients, or would you rather strike out for yourselves?" "Please, pa," crooned Little Willy, "we'd rather strike—wot ho!" "Yes'm," lisped Tiny Tim, "but we'll be on our own; we've had some of your advice, and it hurts."

2. "Tiny," gurgled Little Willy, "now we're on the warpath like the old 'uns, we shall have to buck up, and beat 'em into fits! Hist! likewise skilence! Yonder comes a bloatered haristocrat. We must be on 'im, Timmy!" "We must!" hissed Tim.

3. The unsuspecting youngster came gradually nearer, and then Tiny and Willy made a spring. "T-er-r-emble, otty one!" they yelled, "for we will 'ave our r-r-revenge! Deliver hup that jam-puff, or take the kinsequences!" "Sha'n't!" said the kid.

4. "Then you must die!" said Tim. "Come hon, Willy; this bold ruffian refuses to obey the commands of the Noble Society of the Secret Himage! Help me to bind him up." "Yow! bor-o-o!" howled the kid. "I'll tell my mother! Booh!"

5. After that they took their helpless victim and bound him to a tree. "Now we must hexecute the fearful dance of death all round him," chortled Willy. "Woo-oo! hi tiddley hi ti! 'ow do yer like that, yer warmint! It's Red Indian, so get yer topknot ready to be scalped!"

6. But a rescue was at hand in the shape of the kid's ma, and so the victim didn't die a dead death after all. "There!" she said (smack! bang!), "'ow do you like that, you murderous villins!" Bang! flosh! cosh! The boys didn't like it at all; but they were too excited to say so. (*Then what happened? See next page.*)

The Funny Wonder 284; 9 July 1898 (Tom Browne)

THE "BIG BUDGET" KID ARRIVES.

Big Budget 91; 1 March 1899 (Frank Wilkinson)

Comic Cuts 344; 12 December 1896 (Tom Browne)

DOINGS AT WHACKINGTON SCHOOL.

BY A SKOLLAR.

THESE PICTURES ARE BY TOM BROWNE, THE POPULAR ARTIST.

1. "We did have a fine lark on the 5th. We had a half-holiday, and me an' the other fellars rigged up a guy in the shed. It looked a proper treat.

2. "Well, in the evenin', Snorter, that's our handy man wot drinks like a fish and cleans our boots and makes the corfee (beastly muck, not fit for gentlemen), staggers inter the shed, knocks ovir our guy, and sinks inter the chare hisself. He was in a drunken stupor!

3. "After we had knocked off evenin' prep, and had lited the bonfire, Basher (that's the bully) shouts, 'Four of you kids go to the shed and fetch the guy!'

4. "We went and fetched it, and, by gum! wasn't it heavy! We got it to the bonfire, though——

5. "And pitched it inter the midst of the angry flames.

6. "But the heat woke up old Snorter (for he it was, gentel reder), and he yells and jumps out of the fire and made a horrible fuss. All the littel kids thort it was a ghost or sumfink, and Mrs. Wiggs—our matron, wot looks after our close—phainted in old Whackem's arms. Lor, how we larfed—afterwards, you bet!"

Further doings at Whackington School will be described next Thursday. Screamingly funny!

Big Budget 21; 6 November 1897 (Tom Browne)

The Halfpenny Comic 27; 23 July 1898 (Frank Holland)

THOSE TWINKLETON TWINS AGAIN.

1. THOSE Twinkleton Twins had collared a monkey from Count Macarooni, the organ-grinder. But why should they go to the mask shop and buy two monkey faces?

2. Now the plot thickens. See, they are dressing the missing link in their togs.

3. And then they just shove it in the kitchen where Mamma is sitting peeling the apples.

4. "Bless us well," says Ma Twinkleton, "wotever's that boy a-doin' of. Theevin' an' upsettin' all them apples, and under me very nose too. I'll larn him.

5. "Come here this instant, you young rampscallion, with yer impidence. We'll see whose master.

6. "Great pippins!! Look at that tail. It ain't one of my twins. It's a monk, that's wot it is.

7. "And there's a couple more of 'em besides. Hellup!! Perlice!! There's a menagerie broke loose."

8. But just then those twins smole rather too loud, and Ma Twinkleton tumbled to the game. "Come this way, you young rascals.

9. "It's lucky we've got that old crate; it'll just do for a cage, and cages is the proper place for wild monks and animiles of that breed." Then those twinlets had to stop there all day instead of going out to play.

Big Budget 138; 3 February 1900

Wilhelm Busch was the founding father of the visual strip cartoon. His contributions to *Fliegende Blätter*, needing no verbal translation, were reprinted around the world: there was a Busch strip in the first issue of *Funny Folks* (7 December 1874). His picture stories for children, the *Münchener Bilderbogen* featuring 'Max und Moritz', were reprinted by Alfred Harmsworth's *Comic Cuts* as 'Tootle and Bootle', and inspired those long-lived American characters by Rudolph Dirks, 'The Katzenjammer Kids'. In turn, Dirks' Hans, Fritz and Mama inspired many British cartoonists to use similar characters (p. 64) and plots (p. 65).

GRANDPA EXHIBITS TREMENDOUS ENERGY FOR HIS AGE.

1. "I FANCY, peeple and Hooligans, it'll repay you to watch this set out. If you do not recognise that I am monkeying with springs, blame the artist—not the goak. Go hon.

2. "Grandpa is asleep. He does likkle else now, being 74, and daft at that. I am still monkeying with springs. Next.

3. "You can guess how daft the man is when a hat like that doesn't waken him. But then, of course, 74 is a great age for daftiness.

4. "Now, then, we're getting into the thick of it, as the fly said, when it let loose with its hands and fell into the ice-cream. I'm simply goin' to drop these cans. Are you ready, Grandpa? He speaks not. He is ready.

5. "Bang!!!!! And at one mighty rush off his feetses, Grandpa went up to the roof. I thort this act would be wurf watchin'," said the kid.

6. And after the aged one had gone up and down about sixty times, and was getting a ned-ache—Granny rushed in and tried to hold him down.

7. But alars! Grandmother lost by a short neck, and the three-score-year-and-ten man bounced out of the district—bang!—smash through the window into the great world——

8. And floated serenely onwards. "Hi! You carn't come that way," yelled the cop. "'Taint legal." "Ain't it?" bawled the kid. "You don't know Grandpa. When he starts to do a fing he——

9. "DOES IT!! So you see the joke ends happily after all, the cause of the happiness being a corporation cart of lime just passing. And when Grandpa's paid for what splashed out he isn't going to be charged for anything else."

Big Budget 184; 22 December 1900 (Tom Wilkinson)

The Comic Animal

Humans were humans and animals were animals in the Victorian comic. The humanised animal, walking on his hind legs and dressed in neat Etons, would not evolve until the Edwardian age. In an era of order, animals were kept in their place, as pets ('Kinkins the Pug', p. 75) or performers ('Signor McCoy the Circus Hoss', p. 68). The wilder animals turned up in one-off appearances, and the most popular of these was the elephant, thanks to the famous Jumbo (p. 67). All the tramp double-acts adopted unlikely pets once 'Chokee Bill and Area Sneaker' had set the trend with their snake (p. 70). Later came their kangaroo (p. 71), the two bears who augmented the team of Macaroni and Spermaciti to 'The Happy Four' (p. 74), Willie and Tim's Gussy the Flea (p. 99), and Frank Holland's wonderful 'Walter the Croc', who ultimately took over from 'Jimmer Squirm and Spooky Sprat' (pp. 72-3).

WHIT MONDAY.
The week's work done, The Family frisketh.

It ofttimes happens childish sport	Then ofttimes Wisdom, linked with Age,
Can make us feel like babes again,	On for a bit o' foolin' feels,
And back the happy season's brought	And like unto the new-born lamb
When we were free from grief and pain.	In mirthful glee kicks up it's heels.

Ally Sloper's Half-Holiday 56; 23 May 1885 (W. G. Baxter)

The World's Comic 75; 6 December 1893 (Alfred Gray)

McCOY AND THE STAGGERS.

1. "WE'D got a nice new poster, a startler it was, and startle it did. It startled the inhabitants of Smelt-harbour, I guv yer my word; they'd never seed nuffink like it afore!

2. "Who was going to be the stag, eh? Why ask? Who do yer think could do the part justice but the Signor hisself. At first, when we was a-tying them branching horns on his top-knot, he seemed as mild as butter.

3. "But when we tried to get him to enter the arena —well, there—he gave trouble, not to say no more.

4. "However, at last he was off. The effect was beautiful. The *Smelt Harbour Safety Valve* said: 'The inhabitants of our historic town injoyed last Thursday a treat both intellectual and t'otherwise— well, the audience was satisfied.'

5. "Well, you see, the hunt was to pass *twice* through the arena. That was the trouble. After the first round, it appears, McCoy turned on the hunters, and they had a bit of a dust up outside the tent, and when they came in a second time——

6. "It was the stag as did the huntin'!"

Big Budget 38; 6 March 1898 (Jack B. Yeats)

McCOY AND THE SCHOLLARDS.

1. "WE was in the act of entering the town of Spankbourne, in Zomerset" (it's the Circus Man talking), "where there's a boys' school—in fact, it's all boys' school. The Signor had his work cut out not ter e⁺ on 'em, and when he sneaked a cake off one of 'em, Oh my! didn't they squalk and vow revenge.

2. "That very evening at the show, one of them little schollards up and offered McCoy a bun—just when he was a-doing his high jumping act, a-flying over five-barred gates like a hangel (which comes before the clownd and the pig playing football act). Well, the Signor took that bun, and, would yer believe it——

3. "It were loaded—yus, loaded with pepp— was the revenge of the schollard." Now what did the Signor do?

4. "Well, he went and stood around outside the school, and the clownd, having first fixed a noose handy, put an ole tin can and some string where the schollards couldn't miss 'em. 'Now,' he chuckled, 'a hoss's tail, a tin can, and some string. They can't resist 'em.'

5. "And they couldn't. In course they was at once for tying that tin can on to the hoss's tail. To do it they had to stand inside the noose, you observe. All of a sudden——

6. "McCoy fetched a jump—they was ————

7. "Well, that sagacious quadrupedlar took them schollards through the back parts of the town where the mud was deepest, and then to the——

8. "River. But one of the schollards cut the rope, sudden—so sudden that the Signor sat down on his nose, which annoyed him; but he was rewarded later on.

9. "You see, when those schollards got back to the sc— house wet, and dirty, there was ructions. A—they lay row a-waiting, McCoy looked in. How's that for rev——

Big Budget 42; 2 April 1898 (Jack B. Yeats)

It was Jack B. Yeats—of course—who created something special out of the animal world. The character he gave to his 'Signor McCoy the Wonderful Circus Hoss' literally bucked off the pages of *Big Budget*, leaving his owner, the Circus Man, standing at the post. The first funny animal hero in comics, McCoy is the undoubted ancestor of such later great haybags as Roy Wilson's 'George the Jolly Gee-Gee' (*Radio Fun*, 1938).

THE ADVENTURES OF CHOKEE BILL AND AREA SNEAKER (continued).

1. "Dear Mr. Edditter,—Yer wanter know 'ow we went on wiv that snike we burgled? Lawst you 'eard it was locked in the celler. Yus! Well, we brung it out, an' tied it to a post in the backyawd ter think erbout it.

2. "Finerly we decided to drownd it. So I puts it in a big back-pocket of a coat an' stawts out.

3. "Orl went well till the snike 'e wriggles out o' me pocket an' pops 'is face out o' the back o' me coat. 'E giv' a gemman wot was jist behind an orful fright.

4. "Well, I tucks 'im in at the bottom o' me coat, an' 'e worms 'isself art o' the back o' the neck an' stawtled a pawty wot'd ony signed the pledge the night afore.

5. "So I farstens up the collar an' kep' 'old o' the coat-tails ter keep 'im in. Wot does 'e do but bite a 'ole froo the middle o' the back, a-horrifyin' of 2 little grocer-boys in so doin'?

6. "At larst we gits 'im ter the river. I wos just perpoundin' ter Area a few rough ideas on snike-drowndin'—

7. "When that there ungriteful sarpint chucks 'isself out like a spring-coil, and shoots me an' Area 'eadfirst inter the sloshy worter—

8. "Where we stuck! Then 'e sot darn an' larfed.—Yer 'umble, CHOKEE."

Comic Cuts.

ONE HUNDRED LAUGHS FOR A HALFPENNY.

No. 428. Vol. XVII.] Registered. One Halfpenny Weekly. [July 23, 1898.

THE ADVENTURES OF CHOKEE BILL AND AREA SNEAKER. (The Training of James Enery the Kangaroo.)

1. "DEER MR. EDDITTER,—Ter go back to my animal-trainin' idea. Lawst week I met a gemman wot 'ad travelled wiv a troupe of performin' fleas, an' 'e sed animal-trainin' wos orl done by imitation.

2. "So when we got 'ome we tried it on James Enery the kangaroo. I wanted ter teach 'im a few intellectooal feets—standin' on 'is 'ead an' walkin' on his 'ands, an' sich. So we stawted a-doin' of 'em ourselves fust to eddicate him.

3. "Well, we put our whole souls inter the tawsk. James Enery looked on a bit, an' then seemed ter weary, an' turned round the other way. We waited abart 10 minits for 'im ter turn back agin, but as 'e didn't do so—

4. "We walked rarnd on our dooks an' did dooty on the other side, so's our example wouldn't be lorst on 'im. 'E looked sorter dreamy, I thort, but we stuck to the work of eddicatin' till we wos nearly black in the face—

5. "Till orl at once James Enery started ter snore, and, gittin' up sudden, we farnd 'e wos farst asleep, an' proberly 'ad been orl the time. Werry disheartenin' it wos, but we worn't ter be dornted—

6. "An' whenever we 'ad a little leisure we follered the kangaroo abart the 'ouse, walkin' on our dooks or standin' on our 'eads. At larst 'e seemed to understand, and stawted a-tryin' and 'e wouldn't give way till 'e could do it.

7. "'E wos at it orl day, an' at night we could 'ear 'im falling erbout the place a tryin' 'ard ter do it. Area yoosed ter wake up terrified. 'E thort it wos burglars, wot 'e's perticklerly nervous erbout.

8. "Finerly, James Enery seemed ter tumble to it, and one mornin' we wos delighted ter come darn an' find 'im standin' on 'is head, like a good 'un; an' as fer walkin' on 'is 'ands, 'e could do it like a bird.

9. "But we wish we'd never started it now, for he's never yoosed his legs since. Now we've started teachin' 'im ter ferget is eddication occasionally, an' sit an' walk as he yoosed to in the parst.—Yer 'umble, CHOKEE." **(Another Set Next Week.)**

Comic Cuts 428; 23 July 1898 (Frank Holland)

THE ASTONISHING STORIES OF JIMMER SQUIRM AND SPOOKY THE SPRAT — NOT FORGETTING WALTER THE CROCODILE.

1. "DEER MISTER EDDITTER,—Take my tip, an' wotever yer do, never sneak a crokkerdial! Yer know that wun as we snook larst week in a sack by mistake? Well, a nice job we've 'ad wiv 'im, I tell yer. Tork erbart a korfdrop. Well, 'e is a korfdrop. 'E seemed 'armless enuff when we got yoozed to 'im, so we let him crorl erbart the place to 'is 'eart's content.

2. "Well, o' coarse, like the rest o' people, as soon as we guv 'im a hinch 'e tuk a yawd, an' when me an' Jimmer wos a-sittin' in the drorin'-room, wot does 'e do but cawmly creep orf darnstares as quiet as a mowse—

3. "An' crorl into the bedroom of a gemman wot lives on the fust floor corled Mister Mopper. At it 'appened, Mister Mopper 'ad cum 'ome wearied out wiv' bizness an' beer an' wun fing an' anuther, an' gorn ter bed. "Wot O!" ses Walter (that's the crokkerdial), as 'e shoves 'is snowt in between the kurtens.

4. "Well, o' coarse, that wornt a crime in itself, but 'e didn't stop there. 'E marches 'isself inter the room an' stawts a-toyin wiv' Mister Mopper's trarsis an' fings wot wos 'angin' on a chare. 'Narce pare o' trarsis these,' 'e chuckles to 'isself. 'Wonder 'ow they'd look on my manly form?'

5. "An' wiv that 'e squirms 'isself up 'em, and wuks 'is way up inter the koat an' weskit. Well, 'e wos gittin' erlong werry nicely, thank yer, when orl of a sudding—

6. "Mrs. Mopper busts in! 'Wot!' she ses, as she seed the toggery wrigglin' erbart on the floor—finkin' it wos 'er 'usband—'Wot! Drunk agane, yoo old repperobate? I'll giv' yer drunk, yoo yooman beer-barrel!'

7. "An' wiv that she whacks inter Walter for all she wos worth. 'Tek that,' she ses, 'yoo walkin' brewerry, an' that an' that!' An', o' coarse, Walter 'ad ter take it. 'Owever, at larst 'e mannidged ter pull 'isself together, an' whips rarnd an' faces 'er.

8. "'Woman!' 'e ses, bustin' wiv' rage, 'ow dare yer biff me wiv' a broom like that? Tutch anutther hare of my 'ead if yoo dare, an' I'll screem an' corl a copper!'—Yoors trooly, SPOOKY THE SPRAT."

Big Budget 181; 1 December 1900 (Frank Holland)

THE ASTONISHING STORIES OF JIMMER SQUIRM AND SPOOKY THE SPRAT, NOT FORGETTING WALTER, THE CROCODILE.

1. "Deer Mister Edditter,—We've 'ad an orful time wiv Walter, the crokkerdial, this pawst week. I reely don't fink we can keep 'im. Corse 'e's a bit o' company for us, an' 'armless enuff in a way, but 'e's so obstropperlus. The other day the milkman left 'is big kan artside the drorin'-room winder.

2. "Well, Walter, as it 'appened, wos just lyin' on the sofer in the drorin'-room, an' 'earin' the kan bein' dumped darn on the pivement, peeps art o' the winder ter see wot wos on. Course 'e spots wot it wos in 'arf a jiff, an' a gleam ov greed kums inter his optick.

3. "'Wot, milk? That bewtiful beveridge of me child'ood!' 'e ejackerlates, as 'e pushes 'is face inter the kan an' niffs the liquid like a firsty navvy smellin' a pot ov beer arter a 'ard day's work.

4. "'Oh, chase me! I'm on it like a burd!' 'e ses. An' wiv that 'e bownces in like a kart-load o' bricks. An' there wos a sound as though sumbody wos pullin' up worter wiv a fousand 'orse power pump.

5. "'Arf a mo' later back comes the milkman, just as the larst bit o' Walter was diserpeerin' inter the kan. O' corse the man knoo nutthink erbart Walter bein' inside——

6. "An' just as the crock 'ad 'is mouth open, an' the milk wos pourin' darn 'is throte, the milkman dips 'is arm in ter ladle sum moar milk art, an' shoves the kan 'arfway darn Walter's throte.

7. "Natcherally Walter did the same as yer'd ha' done yerself—'e snapped 'is jawrs to, an' bit the pore man brootal. It wos 2 foot long that bite. It started at 'is finger-tipps an' ran rite up parst the elber.

8. "Well, as ennybody knows, there ain't no pleashure in bein' bit by a krokkerdial. The pore feller neerly yelled the street darn. Bime bye, arfter neerly pullin' the man 'ead-fust inter the kan——

9. "Walter 'avin' got some of 'is own back, let go, an' bobs up sudden like a rokket. When the milkman seed 'im, 'e neerly went orf 'is onion. Just then we 'ears the row an' rushes up.

10. "'Walter!' I yells, 'wot are yoo a-doin' of in that milk-kan? Didn't I ferbid yer to go outside the 'ouse?' Well, as soon as 'e 'eerd my voice 'e flopped darn inter the kan like a shot.

11. "'Cum out, sir, this minnit!' I ses, as we jumps darn onter the pavement. 'E wouldn't cum at fust; 'e sed 'e 'adn't finnished orl the milk. But we wos firm wiv 'im, an' at larst got 'im out.

12. "An', as I karried 'im in, I guv 'im a good torkin' to. 'Walter,' I ses, 'why are yer sich a worry? I do wish yer woodn't be so obstropperlus!'—Yoors trooly, Spooky the Sprat."

Big Budget 182; 8 December 1900 (Frank Holland)

JOKES

Use VICKERS' INKS! **Use VICKERS' INKS!!**

½D ½D

With which is incorporated "THE JOKER."

No. 1.—Vol. I.   Thursday, January 20, 1898.   One Halfpenny.

1. "Macaroni," said Spermaciti, "can dat be beer?" "How can I tell till I've tasted?" said Mac.

2. They tasted. All four of them tasted several times, and when they were sure it was beer, drank more.

3. "We'll teach 'em," said the Force, disgusted at the loss of so much good liquor.

4. "Dilute it. Mix it with water. Souk 'em through," said the Force.

5. But when those four were freshened up, they were altogether too lively.

6. And when last seen were wearing the helmets and tunics of the defeated Force.

Prize Page, No. 8.   Lots of Prizes.

Jokes 1; 20 January 1898 ('M.A.B.')

EXTRACT FROM THE DIARY OF KINKINS THE PUG.

1. "3 p.m.—Round the houses with 'our kid' and little Johnny Fauntleroy. We stop outside a shop where Jeddah, the Derby winner, is on show. Looks as if butter—let alone *Cheddar*—wouldn't melt in his mouth. I wonder what those funny things are it's standing on?

2. "3.30 p.m.—The kid and Johnny are making a Derby winner for themselves. It's Billy—so named because he has whiskers (Billi: ancient goatese word, meaning whiskers). I begin to have a suspicion that Jeddah was a rocking-horse, and that Billy is to be one (beg pardon, rocking-goat).

3. "3.30½ p.m.—Little Johnny Fauntleroy has got the hump badly—not his own, but Billy's. Tommy seems to be enjoying himself; evidently the hump isn't catching. I'm afraid Johnny will fall. But he needn't be so frightened; I'll catch him.

4. "3.30¼ p.m.—Billy is skating round the garden, so is Johnny. He is holding on frantically to Billy's whiskers. (I forgot to tell you that Billy has whiskers all over him.) I am wondering if it would be well to bite whiskers. It's a good thing Billy keeps his hair on, or where would Johnny be?

5. "3.30½ p.m.—Things are getting mixed. I have just remembered an urgent engagement, and the Kinkinses are renowned for their punctuality. Jeddah-Billy has just caught Johnny a back-hander. Tommy is still laughing like a bagpipe.

6. "3.31 p.m.—The laugh has ended in a wrong note. Billy has charged Tommy worse than a magistrate, and without the option of a fine, too. I am not surprised that Jeddah won the Derby now. If it can hop about on those rocker things anything like Billy it will win anything."

Comic Cuts 428; 23 July 1898 (A. H. Clarke)

ROYAL SPORTS IN THE CANNIBAL ISLANDS.

1. The Tinkeroo Island Annual Athletic Meeting took place before the king last week. The meeting opened with a glove contest between Blakasinky and the elephant Jumbo junior.

2. And although it came as a surprise Jumbo junior was knocked out in the third round.

3. The next event was a cycle race. Pongo the monkey took the lead at first.

4. This event, however, was won by a neck by the giraffe.

5. A tug-of-war then took place between niggers and animals.

6. But the rope broke, and the king and his suite got so mixed up that the sports came to an abrupt termination.

Illustrated Chips 361; 31 July 1897 (S. W. Cavenagh)

The animals of an expanding empire inspired a mere handful of miscellaneous strips, but in them may be seen the seeds of such humanised heroes as 'Tiger Tim and the Bruin Boys' of the Edwardian era. Animals are on a par with humans, albeit black ones, in S. W. Cavenagh's 'Royal Sports in the Cannibal Islands', a middle page filler from *Illustrated Chips*.

NEVER CHALLENGE A BIGGER MAN THAN YOURSELF.

1. LAST week, in Beebeeland, Mr. Monk, who's getting a dab at cricket, challenged Mr. Sidewhiskers, the tiger, to a match.

2. Then the match started, Mr. Sidewhiskers going in first. "Play," shouted the umpire. "Oh, I shall bowl yer this shot," chortled the monkey.

3. But the first ball caught the tiger in the optic, and he said some very naughty words and began to lose his temper.

4. But the next ball was a fair corker, and bowled him all over the shop. "How's that, umpire?" "Out!" yapped the umpire, and skedaddled, like the wise umpire he was.

5. "Out! is it," growled the tiger. "I'll out yer, you long-tailed, nut-cracking baboon."

6. And ten minutes afterwards the tiger was heard to ejaculate: "Well, people, I fancy I won that match after all. That chap *was* joocy—real joocy, gents."

Big Budget 168; 1 September 1900 (Tom Wilkinson)

Three years later the animals have taken over; there is now no need for a supporting cast of humans. 'Never Challenge a Man Bigger Than Yourself' is still in the filler category, but is set in 'Beebeeland', *Big Budget*'s private comic colony somewhere in the Dark Continent. This idea was lifted from *Comic Cuts*, whose own comic colony was colonised six years earlier, but which was essentially human (p. 112).

The Comic Age

The Victorian Age, unmatched in exploration, invention, and ceremony, was caught in its comics to a surprising degree. Surprising, because to us, today, the comic is an entertainment for juveniles. Both the Queen's Jubilees, 1887 and 1897, were celebrated in the comics (pp. 79 and 82), as was her Birthday (p. 83), her country home (p. 80), and her Memorial to her Consort (p. 81). Victorian personalities turned up in comics: the Prime Minister (p. 84), the leading stage knight (p. 85), and the favourite comedian (p. 86), who was soon given a whole comic paper of his own (p. 87). Tom Browne delighted in topicality and placed his 'Airy Alf and Bouncing Billy' at every national sporting event. Riding the bicycle boom, Alf and Billy also pioneered the latest forms of motorised transport (pp. 96–7).

CHRISTENING OF JUBILEE SLOPER.

"With his well-known fondness for little children, Albert Edward stood Sponsor for Jubilee, who was Christened the other day by the Family Chaplain. On account of Jubilee's inherited dislike for Water, the Chaplain performed his functions in a somewhat flighty manner. Poor Pa got a good sprinkling, and Ma could scarcely hold the Muscular Child. During our inspection of the Silver Mug, given by The Prince, those dreadful Boys behaved outrageously."—TOOTSIE.

Ally Sloper's Half-Holiday 148; 26 February 1887 (W. F. Thomas)

Ally Sloper's Half-Holiday 164; 18 June 1887 (W. F. Thomas)

Larks! 24; 9 October 1893 (George Gordon Fraser)

Larks! 27; 30 October 1893 (George Gordon Fraser)

Big Budget 1; 19 June 1897 (Tom Browne)

Vol. VI. No. 154.   WEEK ENDING SATURDAY, MAY 26, 1900.   PRICE ONE PENNY.

AIRY ALF AND BOUNCING BILLY SPOOF THE BARMY ASYLUM PEOPLE.

1. "BROKE agin," murmured a voice—it was that of Airy Alf. "As broke as Kruger's smeller," moaned another voice, which belonged to the one and only Bouncing Billy. "Wot's ter be done?" groaned Alf. "Oo's ter be done, you mean," purred Billy. "Har, har! a nidear! Look at that notis." And the plot was plotted there and then.

2. "'Ow do I go now?" squeaked Billy. "Jist a litt'e more on that pimple on yer boko," prattled Alf, "and you'll lo k a biger ijiot than nacher made yer." "None o' yer check," growled Billy, "or I chucks the job." And, for a moment, it looked like another row between the bounders, but Alf rammed the paint brush in Billy's mouth, and crooned, "I was only chaffing yer, pudding hed. Come on. Let's git yer chains on."

3. Of course you see the game now, dear reader. We thought you would. Ah, what will they be up to next, as you say? To resume. "Bless yer, mum," gurgled Alf, to an old girl standing by, "there ain't no occasion ter be alarmed. I've gottim hunder pu'fect control. Wot made 'im mad, mum? 'E was earst hon a dessert island wiv nuffink but Kromic Cuts ter read for six months. 'Nuff ter make anyone barmy, ain't it?"

4. "Thankee, sir," chortled Alf, "I capchered 'im jest by the duck pond in Hyde Park, arfter a desprit struggle ov 4 days and an arf. Keep 'im safe, sir. 'E's werry wiolent, and if he eskcapes agin jist wire for me, care hof the Dook of Barking, 13, Marlborough Palace."

5. Five minutes afterwards, of course, the terrible fraud was discovered, and a figger shot out of the barmy asylum like a penny rocket. "It's werry forchenate," murmured Billy, "that I took the precorshun of padding me pants wiv ten pounds of sofa stuffing, 'cos these 'ere asylum chaps don't 'arf know 'ow to use those number seventeen trilbies of theirs. Nar fer a nice sorft bit of pavement to fall on and I'm orl rite."

6. Then, after dividing the spoil, the two bounders rigged themselves out and went off to the Exhibition. "Flossie," murmured Billy, to the pretty waitress, "bring hus another bottle of the same as before. We've jist bin ter see our ole pal, Cecil Rhodes, and 'e's given hus a couple o' pounds ov diamonds each fer showin' French 'ow ter relieve Kimberley."

Big Budget 154; 26 May 1900 (Ralph Hodgson)

Big Budget 30; 8 January 1898 (Tom Browne)

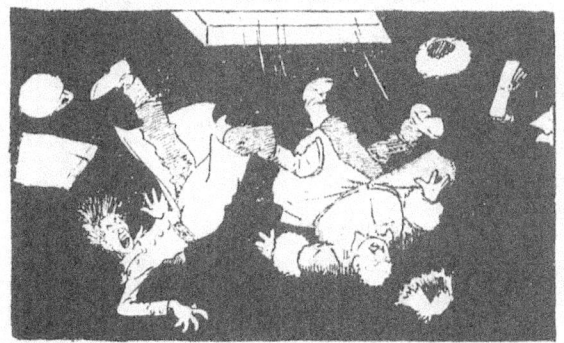

Big Budget 37; 26 February 1898 (Tom Browne)

Big Budget 33; 29 January 1898 (Tom Browne)

Dan Leno's Comic Journal 43; 17 December 1898 (Tom Browne)

Big Budget 5; 17 July 1897 (Tom Browne)

Big Budget 35; 12 February 1898 (Tom Browne)

Big Budget 58; 23 July 1898 (Tom Browne)

Big Budget 106; 24 June 1899 (Ralph Hodgson)

THE BOAT RACE Nº 3
Big Budget 1d

Vol. VI. No. 146.   WEEK ENDING SATURDAY, MARCH 31, 1900.   Price One Penny.

AIRY ALF AND BOUNCING BILLY GET INTO WOE AND TROUBLE AT THE BOAT-RACE.

1. The two cheeky bounders were swaggering along by the training quarters of the Oxford crew. "They all think I'm the Hoxford stroke," sniggered Alf. "Think you're Charley Peace," prattled Billy. "It's me they've got their peepers on. They know by me figger that I'm a regular atlete."

2. "Pip, pip," tootled the pair. "Coming our way, duckies. We're just goin for a quiet walk afore the race. Come and 'ave a plateful of winkles round the corner just to wish us luck." And the two 'Varsity fellows murmured: "Sorry to interrupt you chaps with our girls but you really must——"

3. Biff—biff—"Go"—biff—whack—"before we use force"—thump. "Yow," wheezed Alf, "me perripopilitus is broken in free places." "Whoo," howled Billy, "wot d'yer mean by takin liberties with us afore we've bin introduced."

4. It so happened that the *Battersea Belle* with a cargo of sticky coal tar happened to be passing by, and the B.B. boys just dropped in. "Ugh," murmured Alf. "I only 'ad breakfast arf an hour ago. I don't want nothink more to eat." "Don't splash me," chortled Billy. "Keep on your own side."

5. They got the hoisting tackle in motion and the noble heroes were pulled forth. "Whaggeror! laffinat," spluttered Alf as the crowd smiled somewhat. "Aincher seen a gendleman afore?" And a muffled voice from beneath the tar murmured: "Whadswon, Ogsford or Gambridge? I've godabob on Ogsford."

6. "Billy," moaned Alf, after they'd spat out some of the tar, "it'll take gallons of beer to git the taste of this 'ere stuff out of me mouth." "Same here," gurgled Billy. "Wot unfeelin cruel brutes them University-fellers is. This 'ere Boat Race is a fraud. It ort to be done away with," wheezed Alf.

Big Budget 146; 31 March 1900 (Ralph Hodgson)

Big Budget 17; 9 October 1897 (Tom Browne)

Funny Cuts 45; 16 May 1891 (Alfred Gray)

HOW THE WANDERING KNIGHT DON QUIXOTE DE TINTOGS AND HIS PAL SANCHO PANZA INVENTED THE FIRST BICYCLE.

1. 'Twas dark, and Tintogs, being weary, lay down to rest under a tree, while Sancho Panza, his pal, sat far into the night cooking and eating a sparrow which he had captured with the aid of a pinch of salt cleverly placed upon its tail. Truly, Tintogs' tin costume made a first-class stove.

2. As Tintogs slept, he dreamed a dream, and in it he saw himself and Sancho, his faithful servant and bottlewasher, mounted upon a fearsome machine. He saw himself conquering fearful foes and rescuing many maidens.

3. When he awoke he straightway set himself to fashion the fearsome thing of his dream. Tintogs surveyed the result of his labour with pride, Sancho with wonder. "Great lollipops! What have the idiots been making?" muttered the old mare, as she poked her handsome dial in at the window.

4. And when those bold inventors rode away together on their tandem, the deserted cattle stared in amazement. "What ho, Polly! look here!" gasped the cat's-meat-man's hope. "They've been and gone and chucked us out of work." "Give us the sack? Not much!" exclaimed the indignant moke. "Let's follow them."

5. Later in the day the intrepid cyclists stop at a wayside inn, and wetteth their whistles. On coming out they witnessed the above scene. The mare and the moke were taking their revenge upon their defenceless enemy.

6. As they rode along later, Tintogs on his steed, Sancho on Pollywog, the moke, Tintogs did swear an oath of oaths. "By yonder setting sun! I swear this day, that from this hour, until I lay me down to die, my only seat shall be my faithful cat's-meat, and if she die I will corpse myself!" And Sancho muttered: "Ditto, I swear!" (*Another adventure next Tuesday.*)

Comic Cuts 443; 5 November 1898 (Tom Browne)

Big Budget 16; 2 October 1897 (Tom Browne)

THREE PAPERS FOR A PENNY!

The Big Budget. 1d

ur First Number made 500,000 people laugh.

Vol. I. No. 3. WEEK ENDING SATURDAY, JULY 3, 1897. PRICE 1D.

THE ADVENTURES AND MISADVENTURES OF AIRY ALF AND BOUNCING BILLY.

1. "Airy Alf knew a man who had a motor-car and wished to try it against a cycle to Brighton. I'll take him on," says Bouncing Billy.

2. And whilst the crafty and Airy Alf occupied the man's attention by talking, the wicked and Bouncing Billy went and bored a hole in the petroleum tank of the motor.

3. They started all right. The motor-man was cock sure of winning. But that's because he couldn't his oil running out at the back.

4. Half way down the petroleum gave out. The motor stopped with a diabolical hiss. And the Airy A. and the Bouncing B. rode merrily on chortling with wicked glee.

5. And when the motor-man got off and found that his tank leaked, and that there was no oil to be until he reached Brighton, he just said a few words that are prohibited in Sunday schools and danced dance of madness and despair.

6. There was nothing for it but to get a horse and take the *horseless* carriage along to Brighton, where the motor man found Airy Alf and Bouncing Billy drinking at his expense. "Alf a mo—tor," chuckled B. B.

Big Budget 3; 3 July 1897 (Tom Browne)

PHIL GARLIC, BONES (the dog), AND BILLY WHISKERS (the goat) START A MOTOR-CAR.

1. "Look 'ere," murmured Phil, as he spotted the superannuated 'tater-can, "wot say f we start a motor-car?"

2. The menagerie said it was a great idea, and then Phil started fixing up. "Now, if you both go underneath," he said, "and I tie you up, you can set the machine going."

3. Then he took the car into the town. "Walk hup, gents!" he howled; "have a ride in the splendidest motor-car ever built." And the gents were on it.

4. Off went the car; and for a while all went well. Then, in the thickest part of the town, Billy and Bones thought it time to show how fast they could move.

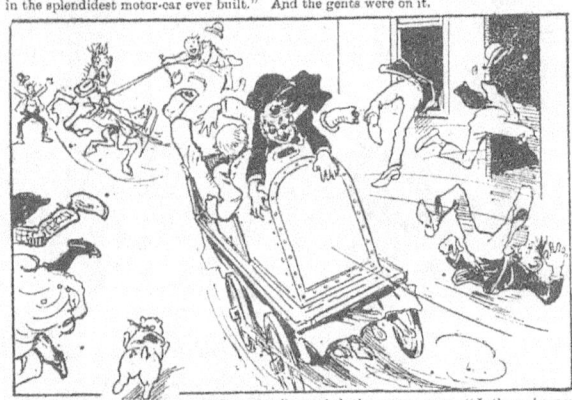

5. And kept on doing so. "Gr-r-r-ip!" gurgled the passengers. "Let's make our wills before we die!" And the crowd smelt danger and vamoosed.

6. But farther on there was a bend in the road that went down-hill, and—whizz! cosh! wallop! Down went the motor into a party of picnickers, who didn't seem to like it somehow.

7. And now Phil is wondering whether Billy and Bones will ever get over it.

HARMSWORTH MAGAZINE JULY 12th 3d ONLY

THE GREATEST JOURNALISTIC VENTURE OF 1898.

The Funny Wonder 284; 9 July 1898

Illustrated Chips 498; 17 March 1900

Illustrated Chips 430; 26 November 1898 (Tom Browne)

THE ADVENTURES OF UNCLE GREENGAGE.

1. OLD GREENGAGE has been getting a bit skittish lately. The other night he went to a music-hall to see the biograph. "Ah've never sin 'em befower," said he, to a young man on his le t, "so ah doan know whether ta expect singers, moosicians, or what.' Then the lights were lowered. "Great Pip! there be a train coming s right for us."

2. Then old Greengage sprang up and waved his red cotton handkerchief. "Hi! danger on the line! Can ye no see the red flag? Hi! hi!" But still the express came on. Really, of course, it was just the biograph picture on the screen, but the old josser hadn't seen a biograph before.

3. "Waal, the boss-eyed gawker's running it, doan take any notice, all make a rush for it." Then the old chap howled: "A'm orf afore I get runned over." And he did run, as you can see in the picture. And the people said things about old Greengage that weren't at all nice.

4. "Ah!" the josser said pantingly, when he got outside the theatre, "that were the narrorest shave of downright decappination ah've ever had. Oi wonder 'ow those other fellows a' git on?"

Big Budget 147; 7 April 1900 (H. O'Neill)

'Weary Willie and Tired Tim' took the air by balloon (p. 99) and the newfangled flying machine (p. 100). The invention of the cinematograph was immortalised by H. O'Neill's countryman-about-town, 'Uncle Greengage', who reacted as did Monsieur Lumière's first startled audience. The annual holidays were always celebrated in the comics, none more so than Christmas. Ally Sloper published his *Christmas Holidays* (p. 102) as a bumper special, extra to his weekly edition. Other comics doubled, even tripled, their standard eight-page issues.

Ally Sloper's Christmas Holidays; December 1887 (W. F. Thomas)

Comic Cuts 32; 20 December 1890

OUR·MERRY·XMAS·NUMBER·ONE·HALFPENNY·ONLY·

The Halfpenny Comic ½

No. 151. Vol. VI.] WEEK ENDING DECEMBER 8, 1900. [ONE HALFPENNY.

BLINKER AND FUZZY-WUZZY DO THE GIDDY GHOST TRICK ON CHRISTMAS DAY.

1.—Hon the nite ov Xmas Eve Fuzzy-Wuzzy, mi slaive, and Hi (Blinker) determined 2 do grate deeds—a serting 'aunted 'ouse 'ad bin loadid wiv grub 4 sum darin' swells 2 'ave thare Xmas dinner thare.

2.—So we thort we wood like 2 investigate the sed grub. Lord! thare woz lots ov it—turkeys, puddin', shampain, hysters, and setterer! "Fuzzy-Wuzzy!" Hi gargles, faintly, "this hiz parrerdice at larst!"

3.—Then Hi 'ad a hidea. "Wiv this yere boar's 'ead," Hi konfided 2 Fuzzy, "we will find the way 2 a slap-up, orlrite blow-out ter-morrer—bein' honly wunst a year!" Then we gouged out 'is heyes and put candles hinside. Nex day noboddy kood find ther boar's 'ead, but—

4.—When ther swells began 2 arrive, 4th kaim Blinker wiv the bons's yead on. That korpsed the footman in livery, 'oo sker-eamed out, "The 'ouse is 'AUNTID!" and—

5.—Nex' minit we woz chasin' them darin' swells all froo the grate park 2 the big gates—orl ov 'em screechin' and yellin' abart terrable ghostesses! Wot woz the sequel?

6.—Bliss and 'armony, o' course! Likewize prime wittles, wich woz heagerly partook ov by ther noble harmy ov tramps and hunwashed, wot the generus Blinker invited 2 partake ov 'is Xmas cheer. O, it woz a tuchin' site 2 see ther gratitood ov them winnin' tramps and 2 'ear them sortly smile at thare good fortin'—so it woz! Tork abart a Merry Christmas——!

The Halfpenny Comic 151; 8 December 1900

Funny Cuts 445; 15 December 1900

The Comic World

The Victorian world was an ever-expanding empire with the Queen a motherly hub. Beyond her bounds, foreigners were even funnier, and Ally Sloper loved to abandon his battered topper and drainpipes to dress up in some hilarious national costume or other. His broken German precedes 'Katzenjammer Kids' conversation by a decade. The international gathering around jolly John Bull for the first issue of *The World's Comic* (p. 107) is a splendid assembly of stereotypes. The funny Frenchman was also a popular butt, thanks to the Paris Exhibition (pp. 108–9), while the Russians provided Anarchists (p. 110) and the Czar himself (p. 111). Yankees were generally sharp con-men (p. 40).

AN EXCHANGE OF COURTESIES—AND DRINKS.

"It is not generally known, but for some considerable time past, Prince Bismarck and Poor Papa have been in daily communication with one another, and when we read of the Prince's resignation in the Papers, none of us were at all surprised that Papa should run over to Berlin. Alexandry was appointed Private Secretary to the Conference which took place, and from him we hear that the crisis in Germany was never once alluded to, the one and only topic being British Gin versus German Beer. Alexandry says that Poor Papa got the best of it, both in the quality of discourse and the quantity of refreshment."—TOOTSIE.

Ally Sloper's Half-Holiday 311; 12 April 1890 (W. F. Thomas)

The World's Comic 1; 6 July 1892

Big Budget 6; 24 July 1897 (Tom Browne)

ALGY ARDUP AND BERTIE BOUNDER AT THE PARIS EXHIBITION.

1. SCENE THE ONTH.—The Paris Exhibition.—Enter two noble British figures. "Ah! there yer are, girls," tootled Duke Bertie Bounder, "I see yer. Meet yer later, duckies." "Pay 'eer," croaked the gendarme at the gate. "Orl right, cocky," yapped Lord Algy, "I'll pay yer. There y'are. Come on, Bertie. Lead me to a refreshment bar. Rool Britannier, and down with French beer."

2. Shortly after the two aristocrats were seated at a table surrounded by waiters. "Wilt quaff the flowing bowl with me, Dook?" quoth Lord Algy. "Odds bodikins," replied the Duke, "I will e'en take a mouthful at thy expense, fair lord." "No, yer don't," growled Lord Algy, "I'll stand a bottle and no more." Waitah! champagne, slave, an' don't blow the 'ead off it." "Oh, zese rich Eenglish," murmured the little French girls, "zey are so charming."

3. But, meanwhile, the two French Johnnies were getting a bit wild at the way the noblemen were mashing their girls, and when they caught Bertie winking at them they got fairly mad. "Sacred blue!" they yelled, "zis ees an insult to France." "Oh, go and wash yerselves," piped the pals. "G-r-r-h! zey 'ave insult us once again. Zey say ve 'ave vash ourselves," shrieked Alphonse. "Nevare!" screamed Henri, and they grabbed the two noblemen by the noses with a big grab.

4. Now, of course, no Briton, let alone a B.B.'ite, would let a Froggie pull his nose, and so in about half a minute there was one of the daisiest scraps going on you'd see in a lifetime. "Let 'im 'ave it, Bertie; goffer 'im! Smash 'im in the duff-box! Bang! Whoosh! Crack!" came from the centre of the crowd, mixed with bottles, bad language, and bits of Frenchmen.

5. And when the fight was over and it was quite safe to come near, two gendarmes came up and marched the Froggies off for assaulting two rich English lords. And, as the two wrecks were carried off to the prison hospital, a small, sad voice moaned "Mon Dieu, Alphonse, vot fools ve vere to touch ze Eenglishmen. Zey fight like devils." "Oh, give me back me right ear," groaned Alphonse.

6. And then the lordlings mounted their trusty motor car and made off (with the girls, of course). "Fair damsel," simpered Lord Algy, "I love yer. Wilt marry me, and share me 'appy 'ome, and me hancestral 'alls?" "Vere are your—vot you say—hancestral 'alls?" asked the simple maid. "Oh—ah—down the Mile End Road, fust turning to the right, past the pub and there you are," guffed the haughty noble. And just then they passed the Froggies. "Solong, cockies," they laughed, "try tatcho for that bald patch on yer heads."

Big Budget 163; 28 July 1900 (Charles Genge)

Big Budget 55; 2 July 1898 (Tom Browne)

THE ADVENTURES OF JIMMY JINGLE AND PETER PENLY.
THEY INTERVIEW THE CZAR OF RUSSIA.

"Here's a pretty jaunt for us," said Jingle; "a telegram from the Editor of *Comic Life*: 'Start at once and interview the Czar on the Peace Question.'" So they decided to disguise themselves as Russian noblemen and proceed at once.

The departure of Count Jimmyniski and Prince Peterova created quite a commotion in the street. Being in a violent hurry to catch the boat train, the driver of the motor-cab started before the Count could get inside.

Arrived at the Czar's palace, they lost no time in seeking an interview with his Majesty. "Bai Jove," muttered Prince P., "these uniforms *do* fetch 'em." "It's our commanding presence," answered the Count, as they passed the bowing flunkeys.

They very smilingly bowed to the Czar when he arrived, but when they introduced themselves and their mission they made rather a mess of it. "P-p-peace, your Majesty," stuttered Jimmyniski, "w-w-we've come to see you about the pleace proposals."

"Police proposals?" said the Czar. "Here, what's the meaning of this imposture? I believe you're Nihilists. Eject these ruffians at once, and cause their immediate arrest." And poor Jimmy and Peter were ignominiously ejected—

And marched off to the police cells. "This here's a pretty way to treat emissaries of peace!" said Peter. "When I get back to England I'll enter Parliament, and propose war with Russia at once." "Wait till you *get* back," moaned Jimmy. (*See how they escaped, in the next instalment.*)

Pictorial Comic Life 35; 25 February 1899

THE SEASIDE SEASON IN COMIC CUTS COLONY

1. The seaside season is on in Comic Cuts Colony. The trains arrive every five minutes, and shoot the people out on to the beach.

2. The hotels are all full.

3. The elephant roundabout is well patronised.

4. Also the band—"The Musical Animals," conducted by Mr. Monkey.

5. The trained whale is doing a roaring business as a pleasure-boat.

6. One has a nasty trick of suddenly diving to the bottom, and upsetting the show. But the passengers are used to his little ways, and being good swimmers, generally manage to get back in time for tea.

The Funny Wonder 237; 14 August 1897

CHURCHWARDEN CHOKER IS SADLY TRICKED BY A DISHONEST BLACKAMORE.

1. Native (catching sight of Churchwarden Choker, who come as a missionary): "A stranger? Good! De Spanish niral got away before I could steal his trowsers, but I l make up for lost time." (Aloud.) "Delighted to meet professah. Permit me to escort yo' to de hotel. Yes, are de Ladrones. Spanish word, yo' know—means thief. Spaniards said we wuz all thieves, so we stole de name.

2. "Allow me to carry your bag, capting. And if yo' will remove your coat and heavy shoes yo' will be much more comfortable. It is so hot. Oh, no—no troubles at all to carry zem!" And Choker innocently handed them over.

3. "That headland, majah, is Procrastination Point, so called because it is de thief ob time. De view is so enchanting, dat when yo' visit it, yo' linger for hours." (Steals his watch.) "Silver watch? Rats!"

4. "Now, honourable sah, if yo' will make yourself comfortle under dis here nice shade, I will carry yo' tings to de tel, and send a carriage for yo'. It's a tiresome walk." "Really," thought Choker, "the natives here are most liging!"

5. Shortly afterwards Choker was disturbed by a gent with a formidable-looking walking-stick. "'Scuse me, sah, but dey's a fellow up at de hotel sez yo' held him up, an' robbed him ob his jewellery, clo'es an' money, an' dere's a gang comin' down to finish yo' off. Gimme dem pants yo's got on, an' skip while yo's got de time.

6. "Run, sah, run! Dere's a hundred years in gaol for any stranger caught stealin' in dese islands. I'll let yo' keep de umbrella—takin' an umbrella ain't stealin' anyway, even in de bes' society." Then Churchwarden Choker made a bolt for his boat.

Comic Cuts 444; 12 November 1898

'The Comic Cuts Colony' was first colonised by *Comic Cuts* on 10 November 1894: four pictures described the Great Mushroom Development. The Colony ran irregularly for years, introducing such occasional characters as 'Smirk the Elephant Detective', a parody of the paper's fictional feature, 'Dirk the Dog Detective'. The series grew so popular that on 4 May 1895, all the comic's strips and cartoons took place in the Colony! Later the C.C.C. overlapped into *Comic Cuts*' companion, *The Funny Wonder* (p. 112). Blackamoors were always good for a laugh, and were popular butts in other strips, such as 'Churchwarden Choker'.

Big Budget 46; 30 April 1898 (Tom Browne)

CHOWGLI AND STRIPES TAKE A DANGEROUS RIDE.

1. "Jee-crikey!" smiled Chowgli, "if dat ain't de biggest winkle I nebber seed!" "Him must hab 'scaped from Barnum's," added Stripes. "Let's take 'im 'ome."

2. So, with a few bits of twine, they harnessed that snail, and got on its back. "Golly!" said the kid, "dis ain't no 'spress train; but 'im goes up hill well."

3. When it took to going up the side of the cliff, though, the little pals were hardly so comfortable. "Somebody git me a bit ob resin, me hands so slipperly!" yelled Chowgli.

4. He didn't require it, though, for the kid managed to grasp that motor-car's rudder. "Dis am a little bit ob nice," said the tiger. "So-so!" answered the Kid. "Take you finger-nails out ob me weskit—dey tickle."

5. But soon afterwards the snail had that tired feeling, and drew in its head and tail to have a snooze. "Berry rude to go to sleep when you got company!" screamed the Kid, as he and Stripes left rather sudden for the earth. "Dis will hurt our feelings."

6. But it didn't, for their fall was broken by two of Mrs. Greaterouselbird's eggs. "Lawks!" it said, "me hab hatched some chicks in me time, but dese two tings take de onion. Me not going to lay no more eggs."

Illustrated Chips 467; 12 August 1899

The opening up of Africa provided plenty of fun and some serial-like adventure for Willie and Tim and Alf and Billy (p. 114). The *Big Budget* boys were usually found in that unlikely area of Africa, Beebeeland, clearly a near neighbour of the C.C.C., as Comic Cuts Colony was colloquially called. The first Negro hero was the well-drawn 'Chowgli', out of Mowgli by Little Black Sambo, who shared jungle fun with Stripes the tiger from 21 January 1899.

ANOTHER LETTER FROM WUN LI, THE CHINEE.

1. "DEAR MR. EDITOR,—I still find dis de most obligin' country in de world. De kindness ob yo Blitish people is simply hebbenly! Fo' instance, de way yo pervide nice cool drinks in de streets for de wayfarers and odder people who am dry is weally lubly. Wo! Me takee dis idea back to China certingly fo' suah! I muchee pleased at Blitish thoughtfulness. Again, Mister Editor——

2. "Oh, de lubly music in de streets! And de obligin' young ladies who askee me to dancee wid dem! I enjoy dis sort ob ting better dan a plate of boiled puppy wid snail fritters around de edges. Wo! It am glorious! De young misses who dancee am so pleasant and kind.

3. "And also, Mister Editor, how kind is de people around Petticoat Lane, hey? I buy one nicee new top-hat fo' two-poun'-ten (dat was made for de Prince of Wales, only it didn't fit proper), and dey den makee me one big present ob a suit ob clothes! Wo! A present fo' nodding—just because I buy one ob de Prince's silk hats! How kind an' simple dese people are, hey? Wo!

4. "But de ting dat impress me most wuz de respect ob de people when dey see me wid my new Blitish clothes on! Dey cheer, and smile loud, and clap me on de back, and hooray! Sez I, dey take me for de Prince ob Wales, because ob dis hat ob his! I do not undeceive dem, but let dem cheer me still muchee! It wuz grand, Mister Editor, and I really proud ob de English people. I really am. Wo! I muchee flattered. — Your hebbenly chop-chop, MISTER GEORGE WUN LI."

Big Budget 180; 24 November 1900 ('Jan')

The Victorian Oriental was not yet the Yellow Peril, and the Cheery Chink and the Jolly Jap were interchangeable objects of amusement. Naturally, the Heathen Chinee was the funniest, because he had a pigtail, although the Boxer Rebellion made him a little less laughable (p. 142). High caste Indians were funnier than low (p. 117), and the Discovery of the Pole was pie to the likes of the rival tramps (pp. 118-19).

1. While Yummisweet, the nurse, was out with the Rajah's son and heir the other day she met a chap that she was sweet on. "Good-morrow, dear," remarked the chap; "the morn is almost as sweet and gracious as thyself." "Oh, go hon!" she smirked shyly. "You don't say so!" But in the meantime Jolop, the black boy, was busily engaged, as you will see.

2. When Yummisweet found she had lost the kid, she went to the Rajah, and tore her hair a bit. "Oh, my lord! my lord!" she said. "thy child hath been pinched!" "W-hat!" yelled the Rajah, "Base woman, thou shalt be slain if he is not found."

3. But before getting on with the slaying, the Rajah thought of the elephant. "Tuski," he said brokenly, "my child hath been nicked! Find him, and your grub allowance shall be doubled." "I will," sobbed Tuski.

4. For many hours the faithful animal mouched round, and at last he came across Jolop and his pal, who were treating the son and heir to a little gentle exercise. "What ho!" murmured Tuski; "I fancy I'm in this."

5. And the joy of the loving father, when his offspring was brought back by Tuski, was too deep for any words except Indian ones—which you wouldn't understand. Poor old Jolop wasn't quite so delighted, though; and neither was his pal.

6. "Ah!" murmured the Rajah a little later, "this is something like. How do you like it, boys? Mustard's a very fine thing, you know. Don't you think so?" The boys certainly differed from the Rajah, but they were too much occupied to say so. Tuski, however, felt pleased with himself, and Yummisweet was happy.

The Funny Wonder 263; 12 February 1898 (Tom Browne)

Big Budget 85; 28 January 1899 (Ralph Hodgson)

No. 528. Vol. XXI. (New Series.) PRICE ONE HALFPENNY. OCTOBER 13, 1900.

WEARY WILLY AND TIRED TIM AT THE NORTH POLE.

1. Sit tight and draw your breath hard! The things in the picture are not dangerous, if you don't annoy 'em. You see, Willy and Tim were panting with a very deep pant after something exciting; and, as they wanted to be as far away from a police-station as possible as well, they just rigged themselves up with a brand-new motor-car, fitted with a cow-and-dog-catcher, and started for the North Pole. "By-by! tooraloo!" sang Willy from behind. "See you when we come back!" "Don't be long!" wept the girls; "we shall be so lonely without you two nice men. Booh-ooh!"

2. Then away went the merry pair, and travelled and travelled till they got among the icebergs. "Pip-pip!" shouted Willy to the French explorers in the sledge. "We're Roberts and Kitchener on the biffbash for the Pole, to see if there are any Boers about; so please be respectful!" "That's it, Willy," chirped Tim; "dig it into 'em! I can see you getting a thump in the lug before you're much older!" Willy's reply melted a lot of the ice; but the motor went straight on, as if nothing had been said.

3. Pretty presently they got off to have a liker at what was which, and, if so, why. "Tim!" jerked out Willy, "there's some nasty, low-minded, jealous folkses been sneaky enough ter discover the Pole before us!" "It do seem so," agreed Tim. "The warmints! But wos Willy and Tim ever done by jest a handful of explorists? Nay; let us wipe them off the earth!"

4. Whizz! Whurrōo! "Pip-pip! Hi-hi!" shouted Tim, as he ran the motor up against their tender parts. "Gerrout the way! D'yer wanter be run over—careless!" "See!" interrupted Willy; "that's wot you git fer bein' tricky!" And he gave a pathetic address to the people in the air, just like a real M.P. "This is where our patent cow-catching, pants-grabber attachment comes in handy!" smiled Tim. Then there were several dull, sickening thudlets, and all was quiet.

5. Of course those chaps were too biffed-up to carry on about it; so the pals gently but firmly collared the North Pole. "This don't seem a werry lovely thing ter come so far arter!" grumbled Willy. "And it are heavy, too!" "Comforfit!" chuckled Tim; "it's worth it. Hold yer end up, Willy boy, and don't let it all the weight on yer pore pal's shoulders!" So they trotted along till they got to Klondike—the place where people tells themselves there's gold—and—

6. Set up a barber's shop. "'Ere y'are, toffs and noblemen!" shouted Willy. "Come and be the only and fustest ter have a shave under the North Pole!" "Yus," put in Tim, "a clean shave for five quid a time—and a toy to the best-behaved gents! Now, walk up—do, afore we git generous, and raises the price!" And those Klondikers just moseyed up and paid. Then the pals sold 'em the North Pole at a bargain, and came home rich.

Illustrated Chips 528; 13 October 1900

The Comic War

The comic war fought between Alfred Harmsworth's Pandora Publishing Company, James Henderson, George Newnes, C. Arthur Pearson, and Trapps, Holmes & Co, was serious business compared with the real thing—as fought on the funny pages. Ally Sloper had been Special War Correspondent for *Judy* in the Franco-Prussian War of 1870, and now that he had his own weekly *Half-Holiday*, naturally he was ready, aye, ready (p. 120). *Comic Cuts* was first to the front with a Grand Military Number (p. 121), and Tom Browne's Alf and Billy, being bicyclists, were quick to join the Volunteer Cycle Scouts (p. 122). They were the first of the few Britons to rush to Uncle Sam's aid in the Spanish–American War (pp. 123–6), and first to take Fashoda in Victoria's own Boer War (p. 127). Their many adventures with Oom Paul were capped only by their old rivals, Willie and Tim, who took Pretoria personally on 21 April 1900 (p. 140).

SLOPER AT THE MILITARY EXHIBITION.

"At the special request of the Committee, Poor Papa honoured the Royal Military Show at Chelsea with his presence the other day. He was accompanied by Mamma, who was awfully sweet as a vivandiere, after the style of Mabel Love, in 'Faust Up to Date.' Papa was perhaps a little too military, but it's all a matter of taste. The Prince of Wales and the Duke of Cambridge received the visitors, and escorted them round the Exhibition. Ma says at times Cammy was quite skittish. Papa says Albert Edward was awfully tickled with a wheeze he told him about Henry of Battenberg. Papa has not told me."—TOOTSIE.

Ally Sloper's Half-Holiday 318; 31 May 1890 (W. F. Thomas)

OUR MILITARY NUMBER.

Comic Cuts. ½d.

THE "MARVEL" GRAND DOUBLE XMAS 1d. NUMBER 1d. Now on Sale.

ONE HUNDRED LAUGHS FOR A HALFPENNY.

No. 346. Vol. XIV.] REGISTERED.   ONE HALFPENNY WEEKLY.   [DECEMBER 26, 1896.

WHO DID HE MEAN?

Officer: "Private Smith, the sergeant says you used insulting language towards him!" T.A.: "I did not, sir. I simply said some of us here ought to be in a menagerie!"

ON PARADE.

Officer: "What do you mean by coming on parade in that state, sir? Why, you haven't shaved, you dirty fellow!" Soldier: "If yer please, sir, I'm growing my whiskers." Officer: "Oh, you are, are you? Well, you've plenty of time to do that off parade. I'd strongly advise you to shave 'em off before you come on. Two days' pack-drill!"

TOMMY ATKINS AND JOHN BULL.

John Bull: "Tommy, old chap, I'm proud of you! We joke at you sometimes, but we'd be a long way behind without you!"

FROM THE RAW MATERIAL.

'Arriet: "Lor'! Bill, I don't 'ardly 'no' yer—yer looks ser bloomin' smart!"

THE ASSASSIN BRAND

Warranted to kill at 1,000 yards!

TOMMY IN THE WARS AGAIN.

1. Maria says, "Go into the garden, Bill, till I've washed up, and I'll meet you there."
2. Sproggins (on the other side of the wall): "What, that darned skunk of a cat out there again!"

3. "I'll give her a skewallop this time, and no mistake!"
4. Tommy thought he was going through Tel-el-Kebir again!

Comic Cuts 346; 26 December 1896

Big Budget 7; 31 July 1897 (Tom Browne)

DON'T MISS THE INCUBATOR COMPETITION THAT EVERYBODY IS TALKING ABOUT.

The Big Budget 1d

FANCY MEETING YOU!

Vol. II. No. 49.   WEEK ENDING SATURDAY, MAY 21, 1898.   Price 1d.

AIRY ALF AND BOUNCING BILLY WANT TO FIGHT THE SPANIARDS.

Big Budget 49; 21 May 1898 (Tom Browne)

NEWSAGENTS know that a bright, attractive-looking shop draws more customers than a dingy one. We have had a number of ornamental show cards printed, which, when hung in a shop, will give it a smart and business-like appearance, and improve trade. On receipt of a post card we will send two of these cards free of charge and by return of post.

The Big Budget. 1d

ISN'T THIS A SPLENDID NUMBER?

Vol. II. No. 50.　　　WEEK ENDING SATURDAY, MAY 28, 1898.　　　PRICE 1d.

AIRY ALF AND BOUNCING BILLY RUN THE BLOCKADE.

1. To get even with Mr. McKinley, Alf and Billy decided to run the Cuban blockade. "Don't this jest remind yer of Margit?" chortled Alf, as he paced the deck of the *Saucy Shrimp*. Billy scanned the horizon. "By gum, there's a hirouclad!" he yelled.

2. It wasn't, though. It was only a vessel with a cargo of Spanish nuts. But when night fell (it falls with a bump in them parts), an American cruiser turned on the limejooce. "See me biff her," laughed Alf. "We are discovered."

3. Boom! C-rash! That Yankee ship biffed first with a shell that startled the blockade runners a bit. "W-o-o-o-o!" shrieked Billy. "These things can bite!" "Never mind," roared Alf. "Just wait till I come down."

4. Both the *Saucy Shrimp* and the bold blockade-runners were looking a trifle the wuss for wear when Alf ran his eye along that gun. "I'll blow that ship ter Klondike," he lisped. "Don't tork," said Billy. "Fire!"

5. And Alf fired. "Seems ter me," remarked the shark to his pal, "there's something coming our way at last. Wunnerful inventions them torpeeders. I'm on that fat bloke wen 'e drops. What ho!"

6. But did those sharks dine off Alf and Billy? Oh no, not a bit! They'd only got to swim ashore, and, when they crawled out and told the Spaniards they'd run the blockade, there were high jinks, you bet. They're going to get a pension now. Hurroo!

Big Budget 50; 28 May 1898 (Tom Browne)

Big Budget 51; 4 June 1898 (Tom Browne)

NEW HAIR RESTORER COMPETITION
The Big Budget. 1d

TWO BICYCLES FOR WEARY READERS.

Vol. II. No. 52.   WEEK ENDING SATURDAY, JUNE 11, 1898.   Price 1d.

AIRY ALF AND BOUNCING BILLY, THE SPIES, SCOOP THE BOODLE.

1. "Prisonairs," said the Spaniard, "you must work ze balloon or a-die! Here is moooch gold, and here is lead. Vich vil you have?" Alf and Billy voted for the oof in a breath. "Potter out," they grinned.

2. And as the balloon drifted through the moonlight towards the American camp, a muffled voice inquired: "Say, Alfy, ain't these smokes all right?" "Prime!" said Alfy. "Good fun this spy bizness, eh?"

3. When the pale dawn broke, they found themselves spotted by the enemy. "Bet I knock a hole in that fat Johnny," said Alf. "Don't kill anybody yet. Give 'em time ter read the handbills," roared Willyum.

4. But the enemy chipped in with a shell which had a very spiteful way about it. "Oh, for the wings of a turtle-dove!" hollered Billy. Alf thought ditto, but said nix.

5. With their usual luck the bounders struck a tree and clung to it like limpets. "Them chaps'll git 'eartburn if they run like that," sniggered Billy. "Let's slither down and find some grub."

6. They slithered. And while the enemy was balloon-chasing they had a high old time in their camp. "Seems ter me," cooed Alf, as they toddled off with the swag, "those Yanks'll know we've been here." "I guess," lisped Willyum. "Wot luck!"

Big Budget 52; 11 June 1898 (Tom Browne)

Big Budget 70; 15 October 1898 (Ralph Hodgson)

Big Budget 90; 4 March 1899 (Ralph Hodgson)

Big Budget 124; 28 October 1899 (Ralph Hodgson)

Vol. V. No. 125. WEEK ENDING SATURDAY, NOVEMBER 4, 1899. PRICE 1D.

AIRY ALF AND BOUNCING BILLY GIVE THE BOERS A GREAT FIREWORK DISPLAY.

1. It was the firework season, so the Budget boys thought they'd leave their rivals alone for a week and call on Kruger. "Wonder if the old cock will recernise us, Billy," chortled Alf. "Not in," purred Billy, who then addressed the crowd: "Now then, people, take yer seats, and don't forget to chuck yer money in the 'ats at the end of each display. English money only taken. None of yer own two pen'orth of silver to the arf-crown spondoolicks. Don't jap't on the rockets, or you'll g t chucked out."

2. Then the number one display was turned on, and Kruger and his pals were pleased muchly. "Goot—goot—darn goot!" they shouted. "Let us have twice some more." "Rightchar," cackled the pals. "The nex one is going to be a real gool 'un—so don't fergit to get the cof re dy when we comes round wiv the colle ckshun box."

3. "Alfred," spike Billy, "we are giving 'em a treat." "Don't they look pleased?" chirruped Alf. There was no doubt about it, too—they did enjoy it. Uncle Paul was so delighted that he borrowed a real English bob from General Joubert, and slung it into the hat. "And now me deer frends," chorused the B.B. boys, "comes the great and final display which will conclude the evening's entertainment. Let 'er go."

4. And when Kruger and Company gazed upon this, the language almost put the fireworks out. "Vare is dose tam scoundrels!" yelled Paul. "Uncle," groaned the others, "dey haf bolted wider oof." "My bob's a goner," moaned Joubert. "I can never get it back from old Kruger." And later on the stars peeped down on a couple of flying forms. "We'll count up the chink at the next pub," wheezed Billy, "Wot a time we've had. It aint often you can do a Boer down for anything." "Not much," puffed out Alf. "If we don't get a medal each for this, I'll never speak to Joe Chamberlin again."

Big Budget 125; 4 November 1899 (Ralph Hodgson)

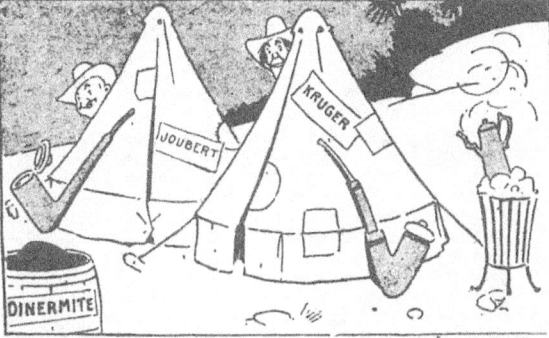

Big Budget 127; 18 November 1899 (Ralph Hodgson)

THRILLING ADVENTURES OF BOUNDERBY BOUNCE, THE WAR CORRESPONDENT.
The Important Dispatch.

1. SINCE sending you my last graphic description of the magnificent victory which I achieved over a powerful Boer force last week, I have been specially selected, on account of the courage which I then displayed, to be the bearer of a most important dispatch. While the troops were eating a splendid Christmas dinner, I was sitting alone at a frugal repast. I scorn to eat while duty calls me. Suddenly, General Buller came into my tent. "Excuse me," he said, "I have here a very important communication to send to General White. I have chosen you, as the bravest man in the camp, to carry it. You may run terrible risks on the journey, but I know you laugh at peril. I can hardly bear to part from you, but duty is duty."

2. After a touching farewell, I left the General and commenced my preparations for the perilous journey. A magnificent steed had been selected for me. Some of the officers tried to persuade me to wear a suit of armour under my clothes. Of course, I scorned to take such care of my life. As I looked at the valuable dispatch I was to defend with my life, I lifted my head proudly, and glanced around with that eagle eye which has struck fear into so many Boers. The soldiers were dumb with admiration at my undaunted bearing. The whole camp turned out to see me off. With a large train of servants I started, amidst rousing cheers from the troops.

3. After many days travelling, I came within a short distance of my destination. The General had presented me with a very powerful telescope before I left, and, looking through this, I saw in the distance a large body of the enemy. Most men in my position would have fled, but not I. "Ha!" I muttered, "here is another chance to show my intrepid bravery. I will secrete myself, and endeavour to overhear the enemy's plans. Where danger lies, there is the heroic correspondent of the *Daily Shrieker*." My servants were trembling with terror——

4. And the whole body fled, leaving me and my faithful steed alone. With the dignity which always distinguishes me, I coolly dismounted, and, first seeing that my horse was safely hidden, I proceeded to take up a most dangerous position, right in the track of the advancing force. My first thought, of course, was for the valuable document on which so much depended. I could hear the enemy advancing close to me; the rattle of their arms and gnashing of their teeth were enough to have frightened many a brave man. But, as I have said, fear is unknown to me.

5. For a long time I heard them moving about in search of me, and I thought of the thrill of admiration which would run through the breasts of your readers as they hear of my daring exploit. Every moment I expected to be discovered, and knew that a terrible death awaited me if they detected my place of hiding. Please bear in mind that nothing but a sense of duty prevented me from springing out and slaying them. After a while, my horse sneezed and—we were discovered. Imagine my astonishment, as, with many bows and apologies, I was requested to come out by—the Boers?—no, by a party of British soldier boys. In my hurry, I had made a slight mistake. It wasn't the enemy after all.

6. Upon explaining that I was the bearer of an urgent dispatch, I was taken before the General. "This is a great honour, my boy," he said; "I have often heard of you, and longed to meet you. Come inside and have a drop of something warm." He then proceeded to open the letter. I cannot, of course, disclose the contents, which were of a very important nature, and referred chiefly to me, requesting that I should be handsomely rewarded. "I should like to give it to you myself, me boy," cooed General White. I am unable, at present, to mention the nature of the reward which I immediately received.

Big Budget 132; 23 December 1899 (Charles Genge)

THRILLING ADVENTURES OF BOUNDERBY BOUNCE, THE WAR CORRESPONDENT.

(Told by Himself and Illustrated by our own Truthful Artist.)

How he was Rewarded by Kitchener and Roberts.

1. Of course, by the time you receive this all England will be ringing with the news that there are now two other great men here besides me. Lord Roberts and Lord Kitchener have joined me. Special instructions were issued to the police not to allow any correspondents to be present at their arrival. Nevertheless, that low truth perverter, Yarnslinger, the war correspondent (ha, ha!) of the *Daily Shrieker*, determined to be there, and hid in a potato sack which was lying on the wharf. But I was there also. Yer faithful Bounderby had his eagle optic on the skunk. Yarnslinger snapped Lord Roberts just as he grasped Lord Kitchener's hand and cooed "Herbert, me boy, Bounderby, you and me'll just give those Boers socks, eh?"

2. At that moment I stepped forth. I could bear it no longer. I felt it was my duty to hand the mangy ink-slinger over to justice. Do not fancy that the fact that th' ugly tramp has repeatedly insulted me had anything to do with my decision. The good of the country demands that the tyke shall be put out of the way. "Gentlemen," I crooned, "it is my painful duty to have to inform you that a spy is present. A French correspondent is concealed——." "Where? Where?" shouted Kitchener, "let's have him shot at once." "Search that sack," I said sorrowfully, for my kind heart ached for the wretched Yarnslinger, scoundrel as he is.

3. In about two twos the soldier boys had the howling Yarnslinger out of his sack by the ear, and one of them proceeded to give him a coat of tar, to keep the damp out, as the two generals had decided to pitch him into the river. I stood and looked sorrowfully on, while Yarnslinger shrieked and raved. The villain dropped note-books and cameras all over the place. The commanders were so enraged that they would have shot him at once, had I not brought my influence to bear upon them. I could not endure to see the wretched creature suffer the fate he so richly deserved.

4. "Now, boys" shouted Lord Roberts, "one, two, three, and away." And two Tommys heaved Yarnslinger into the water. "Oh, let me orf," he screamed, "I won't do it again. I will be good. The doctor said a bath would kill me." But in he went. What a contrast between this poltroon and your heroic correspondent. Had I been in his place I should have met my fate boldly and fearlessly, without a word. I have never known fear. But, there! we cannot all be brave. As I watched him I thought of the insults he had heaped upon me, and——

5. Suddenly Lord Kitchener turned to me and said, "And who are you, sir, to whom we owe our lives? That noble face! I seem to have seen it somewhere. I cannot be deceived. Are you a prince in disguise, or only an earl?" "My lord," I answered, "you may have heard of me. I am the bravest, fiercest fighter in the British army. You have heard of the battles I have won, of the prisoners I have taken. My name is"—(and here I forgot Lord Kitchener's aversion to correspondents and gave myself away)—"my name is Bounderby Bounce. I——" "Wha-at!" shouted Kitchener, "Bounce, the distinguished war correspondent!!

6. "You go after your pal." He was right. Just at that moment a last despairing wail came from the wretched Yarnslinger. Could I leave him to drown? No! Where danger is there am I. Kitchener was right. I would go after my pal! With one bold plunge I struck the water amid murmurs of admiration and rousing cheers. With tears in their eyes, both commanders themselves assisted me. After a fearful struggle with the rapid river (I was under water 37 minutes 26½ seconds at one time), I at last succeeded in rescuing the wretched Yarnslinger, amid the cheers of the soldiers on the wharf.

Big Budget 136; 20 January 1900 (Charles Genge)

Big Budget 137; 27 January 1900 (Ralph Hodgson)

Illustrated Chips 486; 23 December 1899 (Tom Browne)

Big Budget 140; 17 February 1900 (Ralph Hodgson)

THE EXTRAORDINARY ADVENTURES OF BOUNDERBY BOUNCE, THE WAR CORRESPONDENT.

(Told by Himself and Illustrated by our own Truthful Artist on the Spot.)

BOUNDERBY TAKES JOUBERT A VALENTINE.

1. ONCE again has your noble correspondent distinguished himself on the field of battle. One more glorious victory is added to the list of his brilliant successes. In an important engagement fought near here, I have again defeated the enemy, and taken a huge number of prisoners. General White found it necessary to send an important communication to Joubert, and requiring a person of unusual intelligence to be the bearer, he, of course, immediately decided to send me. "But then, supposing I were sent, what would the garrison do without me, in the event of the enemy attacking Ladysmith in my absence?" This consideration alone made me unwilling to set out, but I was at last *persuaded* to go, and the boys gave us a splendid send off.

2. The heat was terrific. The ground was so hot, that every time my foot touched it the boot-leather began to burn. In consequence of the awful heat, my head was fearfully swelled. [It's been like that a long time.—ED.] And my feet were so blistered that I was scarcely able to walk (the magnificent charger which the General had presented to me for the journey had been *burnt up* by the sun). At last we stopped to rest. I had some cold tea with me, but as there was only enough for one, I, with my usual generosity, gave it all to Inki. It was at this time that the scoundrel Yarnslinger, who had been following us, crept, unobserved, through the reeds behind me (as I was told afterwards), and stole the important letter, substituting for it one of his own.

3. Shortly after I arrived at the Boer camp, where I was received with great respect by General Joubert. It was curious to see the fear which my presence caused among the rascals. Drawing myself up to my full height, and casting around me a haughty glance from my eagle eye, I handed the letter to Joubert, I being ignorant, of course, of the dastardly treachery of the cowardly skunk who calls himself Yarnslinger. Joubert was in an extremely bad temper, having received a nasty message from Kruger to the effect that unless he could do something better than hang about *outside* Ladysmith, he'd better chuck up his job. He held out a very dirty paw, and I passed over the letter to him.

4. He opened it and gave a frightful howl of rage. Yarnslinger had substituted for General White's letter one containing a valentine—a fairly truthful portrait of Joubert himself. "Donnerblitzen! Thunderweather!! Beeanskittles!!!" he roared. "This vas meant to insult me, so it vas. I let you know I'm Joubert, the greatest general in the world. Yah!" All this time I stood calm and fearless, knowing that at any moment the thousands of rifles levelled at my beautiful head might be discharged. Ever thoughtful of those weaker than myself, I placed Inki behind me, that the bullets might strike me first. Even the Boers were overcome with admiration at my undaunted bearing, and hesitated to fire.

5. Suddenly I remembered that we, knowing that the flag of truce might not protect us, had brought with us two large squirts filled with soap and water. At that moment Joubert gave the order to fire, and the whole commando let fly at us; but simultaneously I discharged the contents of my squirt full in Joubert's face. He leapt into the air with a fearful scream of agony. Although the Boers had never seen any soap and water, they had heard that the British executed Boer spies by washing them; and the appearance of this novel weapon filled them with terror. Volley after volley we poured into them, and finally the whole commando took flight, leaving thousands lying in terror and agony on the ground.

6. Do not, however, imagine that I had not suffered in this glorious engagement. On the contrary, I was literally riddled with bullets. Inki, who was standing behind me, and consequently escaped unhurt, assures me that he watched the whole fight through a hole in my chest, caused by a large shell. However, I am happy to say I am rapidly recovering. When, late that night, we marched into camp with 10,000 prisoners, we were greeted with such cheers as have probably never before been heard in South Africa. I noticed the traitor Yarnslinger hiding in his tent. I shall really have to chastise the low hound. I am the hero of the town, and every girl in the place is madly in love with your noble correspondent.

Big Budget 140; 17 February 1900 (Charles Genge)

Big Budget 141; 24 February 1900

OUR GREAT PATRIOTIC STORY. See Page 3.

No. 500. Vol. XX. (New Series.) [Entered at Stationers' Hall.] PRICE ONE HALFPENNY. [Transmission Abroad at Book Rates.] MARCH 31, 1900.

1. Poor Boers! Their luck was dead out, but worse was to come when Weary Willy and Tired Tim turned up at the front in their new motor-car. You see, they had come across to capture Kruger, and that's why Tim is got up as a Dutch maiden and Willy as a Boer cornet. "Good luck to you, old coughdrops!" shouted the Tommies, "and don't lose your fizwigs!" "Listen to that!" cooed Tim. "It must be my handsomeness that attracts them." "You—oh, yes!" sniggered Willy; "you're as handsome as a tame faggot—my word!"

2. Still, pretty presently they got to the Boer camp just after old Kruger had finished his tea and winkles. "Ach! vot you call dis, mine leetle fat vrouw?" asked Uncle Paul, pointing to the motor. "Oh!" chimed in Tim, "that's something we found on the kopje—I mean sjambok—no—trek, veldt, rooinek, or blinkin' something—while the British Army was cutting off home. Goes all by its lone, without a single shove. You come and have a canter, Uncle." "Vell, I tinks I dakes a short stroll in dat," replied Kruger; "I vill get mineself inside."

3. "All aboard! Let her went! Pip-pip!" "Yow-oo-ooh! Vot der periliceman vos you doin'?" howled Uncle Paul. "You shdops dis ting immediatvonce, I toles you; an' I vos get oudt!" "Oh, yus, you nice, whiskery old gentleman," smiled Tim; "you'll get out presently—and suddint-like, too! Coo-ho!" "My opinion 'xactly!" piped Willy. "And tell that chap at the back to sit down, or he'll catch a draught in his coat-tails!"

4. How does this suit you, Uncle?" chuckled the pair, as the motor slid down the kopje. "Shakes yer orange free states up a bit, don't it?" "Oo-er! I vos tole you I don't like him," yelled Paul. "Vill you save dis old man, und I vos give you twopence?" "Go long, you silly little silly!" giggled Willy; "you ain't worth so much. You'll find that you'll be owing a bit when you come to settle up."

5. Sw-oo-sh! Kersplash! The car struck the river and shot straight across to the other side, where the Tommies were in waiting. "Ach! mine goot gootness!" yelled Uncle. "I vos a brisoner taken sometimes, aindt it?" "That's so, cocky!" chuckled Willy, "and they've got a few old scores to settle up with you—don't you fret. Now then, out you come—all of you!"

6. Then they stuck the old gent on a Neddy, and took him up to see the British generals. "'Twas me alone wot did this thing!" sang Tim. "Ditto repeato exactlio," piped Willy. "And if we don't get General Buller to stand a tripe supper on the strength of it—well, there'll be trouble for readers of CHIPS to look upon.

(Don't miss our next number—it will be a corker.)

Illustrated Chips 500; 31 March 1900

Illustrated Chips 503; 21 April 1900

10. And later on the pals opened the gates to let in the British Army. "Wotto! Bobs, me boy! come along in and make yourself at home," said Willy. "Much obliged, I'm sure," smiled our champion general; "and if you don't mind I'll ask all my boys in with me to take a muckle o' pinkle with you." "Why, certainly," chirped Tim. "Let 'em all come."

11. And wasn't it fun when the Boer Army, after finding they had been spoofed, returned, to find the British in possession! "What's the game?" asked Tommy Atkins, when Boer tried to climb the wall; "this is the Queen's private property." "Ach! is dot so?" howled the other Boers; "den der game vos oop, and ve trusts ole Kruger never no more."

12. Then the band played, and up went the British Flag with cheers. "Timmy, my noble friend," said Lord Rober afterwards, "I appoint you Governor of Pretoria at thirty bo a week. And your old pal Willy is made Chief Officer of th Canteen." (But in next week's CHIPS you'll find them back home again playing up their monkey tricks as usual.)

The comic peace was short-lived. Within the year, Willie and Tim were off to have a punch-up with the Boxers (p. 142). The century turned and was duly celebrated by *Big Budget* (p. 143), but seventeen days later the Queen was dead. The Edwardian era had begun: would it turn out as predicted (p. 144)?

The Comic Artist
(index to artists)

Baxter, W. G.   2, 66
Browne, Tom   1, 3, 17, 28, 29, 30, 48, 53, 59, 61, 62, 82, 84, 85, 86, 87, 88, 89, 90, 93, 95, 96, 97, 100, 108, 110, 114, 117, 122, 123, 124, 125, 126, 135

Cavenagh, S. W.   50, 76
Chasemore, Archibald   5
Clarke, A. H.   46, 52, 75

Duval, Marie   26

'F.L.'   20
Fraser, George Gordon   57, 80, 81

Genge, Charles   37, 54, 109, 132, 133, 137
Gray, Alfred   42, 43, 56, 67, 94

Hill, Roland   18, 19, 21
Hodgson, Ralph   4, 22, 25, 31, 47, 83, 91, 92, 118, 127, 128, 129, 130, 131, 134, 136, 143
Holland, Frank   32, 38, 39, 49, 63, 70, 71, 72, 73

'Jan'   116

'M.A.B.'   74

O'Neill, H.   101

Thomas, W. Fletcher   27, 55, 78, 79, 102, 106, 120, endpapers

Veal, Oliver E.   19

Wilkinson, Ernest   24
Wilkinson, Frank   44, 60
Wilkinson, Tom   65, 77

Yeats, Jack Butler   40, 41, 45, 51, 58, 68, 69
'Yorick' (see Hodgson, Ralph)

Illustrated Chips 518; 4 August 1900

Vol. VIII. No. 186.   WEEK ENDING SATURDAY, JANUARY 5, 1901.   PRICE ONE PENNY.

ALF AND BILLY TRY TO CELEBRATE THE NEW CENTURY BY BEING VERY, VERY GOOD. WHAT HO!

1. "ALF," sighed Billy, "them there goody-goody-come-and-kiss-me kind of books says if yer good yer 'appy. I've turned over a few leaves in me time at the noo year, but this is the fust bloomin' noo century I've ever struck. I mean ter go straight. Don't the werry thort make yer 'appy?" And Alf said, "C-C-Course it d-d-does, chump 'ead. Carn't yer 'ear 'ow I'm larfin'?"

2. And, my gracious, didn't they start a treat! "Chuck 'em orl on," cackled Alf, "and we'll 'ave a howlin' bonfire. I ain't goin' ter smoke, or drink, or bet, or use norty words never again. Oh, don't I feel 'appy!" "Me too," sighed Billy, "only I fink we'd better drink this fizz, 'cos it might put the fire out, and coals is dear." "Dump it hon" roared Alf.

3. Oh, it was a lovely couple of leaves that they turned over. That same night they strolled into the "Pork and Gridiron" and called for teetotal gargles. Who should be there but Bogey Bertie and 'Appy Ike, swigging beer. "Alf," sighed Billy, "jest look at them there depraved wretches. 'Ow's yer lemmingade?" "Oh, grand," sobbed Billy. "It's—bootiful—so c-c-coolin'!"

4. Don't shudder, reader, please don't shudder. They actually were so good that they went to work! "Ain't it lovely, bein' good?" panted Alf, as he tried to bore a hole in a chunk of granite. "Don't it make yer 'appy?" "Oh, be-yoo-tiful," moaned Billy. "I do love it, Alfy, only I wish I'd got me gloves, 'cos this 'ere job's raisin' blisters."

5. Then the next day came on its hind legs, and that stout gent floated past with the oof in his pocket. And when they'd got over the shock a bit Alf lisped, "Billy, we've been good for free days, ain't us?" "Wo 'ave! What ho!" "That bloke 'ad a red nose, 'adn't he, and 'e'll spend all that oof in drink. Let's rescue 'im!"

6. They did—at least, they rescued the notes out of his right-hand pocket. Two hours later Alf murmured, "Billy, old hoss, this is the 'appiest moment of me life. It makes me swell wiv pride ter fink we've saved that fat cove from a drunkard's grave. Oh, we *are* good. Good 'ealth fer 1901, readers, and don't fergit us on the front page. We'll just hum, cockies."

Big Budget 186; 5 January 1901 (Ralph Hodgson)

NO MORE NOISE THEN.

1. In the next century when all noises in the streets have to be done away with, we shall have noiseless German bands with muffled instruments.

2. And the costers will all have to be gagged.

3. Pa will read his Big Budget in peace then, 'cos all the kids will have to cry into the patent household noise tank.

4. Of course all the traffic will have to be silent. No wheels for the carts, and patent spring pads for horses' feet—not much noise then.

5. Polly will have to shut up, too.

6. Bobbies will carry the silent truncheon so that they won't make a noise when they hit you.

Big Budget 24; 27 November 1897

The Fête held at Mildew Court on Christmas Day for the benefit of the "Asylum for Orphan C... will stand out as one of the most brilliant functions of this remarkable year. It is true, the gathe... was not entirely for the sake of charity, for in many respects it was very like the usual Christ...

Ally Sloper's Christmas Holidays; December 1897 (W. F. Thomas)

STMAS JAMBOUREE.

CHRISTMAS 1897.

...arty given at the residence of the Eminent Littérateur. Still, the cause of the Orphan Cats was
...t forgotten, and it is fondly hoped that when the collecting boxes are opened, something more than
...ouser-buttons and cough lozenges will be found in them.

For Product Safety Concerns and Information please contact our EU representative GPSR@taylorandfrancis.com
Taylor & Francis Verlag GmbH, Kaufingerstraße 24, 80331 München, Germany

www.ingramcontent.com/pod-product-compliance
Lightning Source LLC
Chambersburg PA
CBHW080939300426
44115CB00017B/2882